STOLEN CHILDHOODS

STOLEN CHILDHOODS

Thriving after Abuse

SHARI BOTWIN, LCSW

ROWMAN & LITTLEFIELD
Lanham • Boulder • New York • London

Published by Rowman & Littlefield
An imprint of The Rowman & Littlefield Publishing Group, Inc.
4501 Forbes Boulevard, Suite 200, Lanham, Maryland 20706
www.rowman.com

86-90 Paul Street, London EC2A 4NE

British Library Cataloguing in Publication Information Available

Library of Congress Cataloging-in-Publication Data
Names: Botwin, Shari, author.
Title: Stolen childhoods: thriving after abuse / Shari Botwin, LCSW.
Description: Lanham: Rowman & Littlefield, [2024] | Includes bibliographical
   references and index.
Identifiers: LCCN 2023044706 (print) | LCCN 2023044707 (ebook)
   | ISBN 9781538183625 (cloth) | ISBN 9781538183632 (ebook)
Subjects: LCSH: Adult child sexual abuse victims. | Post-traumatic stress disorder. |
   Psychic trauma.
Classification: LCC HV6570 .B66 2024 (print) | LCC HV6570 (ebook)
   | DDC 362.76/4—dc23/eng/20231005
LC record available at https://lccn.loc.gov/2023044706
LC ebook record available at https://lccn.loc.gov/2023044707

♾️™ The paper used in this publication meets the minimum requirements of American National Standard for Information Sciences—Permanence of Paper for Printed Library Materials, ANSI/NISO Z39.48-1992.

This book is for you, buddy boy! It was not until I became your momma that I realized I am so much more than a childhood abuse survivor. Parenting and loving you has proven to me that we can break the cycle of abuse. You are a beam of light, joy, and happiness.

CONTENTS

Introduction

For over twenty-five years, I stayed silent about my history of childhood abuse. In fact, for most of my childhood and early adulthood I had no conscious memory that anything had happened to me. I always knew something was wrong in my family, but I had no words or ways to describe my feelings. I started working in the psychology field immediately after I received my master's in social work. Months later I started working as a group therapist in a renowned center for eating disorders, Renfrew Center. Most of the residents checked into this facility because they had a raging eating disorder that was ruining their physical and emotional well-being. Every day I ran these groups, residents were talking about their history of surviving some type of childhood abuse. One young woman in her early twenties told the group that the only way she was going to be able to recover and let go of her eating disorder was if she began dealing with the sexual abuse by her swimming coach as a child. Another resident in her late fifties shared that she lost decades of her life in adulthood after burying years of physical abuse done to her by her father.

After working at Renfrew for a couple months, I noticed a shift in my personality. I became withdrawn. I had panic attacks when I left work for the day. I sat in my apartment and just stared at the walls at the end of each day. I started avoiding contact with my family. While I did not speak a word about my abuse, I was able to tell my supervisor that I felt depressed and overwhelmed. I told her that I had also struggled with eating disorder behaviors starting around the age of thirteen. I was able to identify that the biggest trigger for me working at Renfrew was hearing about residents who had been abused as children. My supervisor asked me if I had a history of trauma or abuse as a child, and I adamantly denied such a thing. I told her I could not relate to these residents and that I felt incapable of helping them. She suggested that I go to therapy. At the time I was mad and defensive, but there was a part of me that felt relieved that someone finally recognized that I was in pain.

For about the next six months, I kept repeating this mantra in my head as I drove to work. I kept repeating to myself, "I need help. I need to tell someone." At the time I was not conscious of what I needed to say. I knew I was falling apart and that I had to do something. After much hesitation and reluctance, I decided to go to therapy.

I met my therapist, Dorothy, when I was twenty-six years old. When she asked me what my relationship was like with my family, I told her, "Oh we are very close. My mom is like my best friend." As I spoke these words, I could feel wrenching pain in my gut. I never told Dorothy what I was feeling in my body. I only talked about the thoughts going on in my head, which usually were conflicted and fragmented.

Months after I lost a close family friend to cancer, my depression worsened. I thought about how this world would be better off without me in it. I felt like my heart was racing and my body was frozen when I spent time with my parents. One day when I went to my parent's house to grab some items for my apartment, I lost it. I ran out of the house, got in my car, and sobbed. It made no sense to me. I had no idea what was happening or where these feelings were coming from. I called Dorothy and told her I needed help. When she called me back and asked me what I needed help with, I could not answer her. I was so confused. I felt like my world was turning upside down. I had no words, but I noticed that my body was feeling all kinds of sensations. At the time I could not speak in words about what my body was trying to tell me.

Days after that episode at my parent's house, I picked up the phone and I left Dorothy another voicemail saying, "I was sexually abused as a child. Someone went inside of me." When I met with Dorothy for our next session after I left her that voicemail, she sat in her chair with tears pouring down her cheeks. I was frozen. I could not feel my body in the chair, and I dissociated my way through that session. I could see that she was concerned about me, but I could not take in the empathy she was expressing. I felt guilty and I felt like I was betraying my parents. I was not able to tell myself or Dorothy who abused me, or how old I was when it started and ended.

Once I broke my silence, my body would not let me forget that I had been sexually abused. Every time I shamed or belittled myself for speaking about the abuse, I had body memories, which is a form of dissociation. I continued seeing Dorothy, but I spent most of my sessions trying to pick a fight with Dorothy to avoid dealing with my grief and heartbreak. I would do anything to make the truth not so. I spent hours each day agonizing as my body felt different sensations from the assaults. I had flashes of my younger self at all different ages. I had memories of being on the playground in grade school feeling disconnected and ashamed. I remembered thinking at different ages, "Someone is hurting me at night." I had flashbacks of being in middle school and wishing the principal would tell me that my parents had died and that I needed to go live somewhere else. I had vivid memories of being a teenager and looking at myself in the mirror in horror. At the time, I saw a young woman that was full of shame and despair. As the memories came flooding back, I began to put pieces of my fragmented life together. I started seeing Dorothy three to four times a week so I could continue processing memories and find ways to keep myself safe. I did not want to go inpatient because I had a dog that I loved to pieces, and I wanted to continue working so I could be financially independent.

I stayed in intensive outpatient therapy for years. I carried around a small notebook that I could write in, so that when the memories, thoughts, or feelings came to the surface I could write them down. It took me weeks at a time to find words and tell Dorothy each time I had a new memory or flashback. I went into depressive episodes, and on many occasions, I called Dorothy and told her I did not want to be alive anymore. There were dozens of sessions when I told Dorothy I wished I had never opened my "big, fat mouth." I felt like a horrible daughter. I felt like a total misfit. I felt ruined.

I continued to go to therapy, but I used every defense mechanism I could to try and forget what I had already remembered. I repeatedly said to myself, "I am a liar," and denied that anything had happened to me. At the time, I convinced myself that Dorothy did not believe me. When I left the therapy sessions I wanted to disappear. I thought of different ways I could end my life. I stopped eating and my sleep patterns were a mess. I had nightmares, flashbacks, and body memories. For several months I would not tell Dorothy who hurt me. I denied that any of the abuse was done to me by my parents. At one point, I told her that I was sexually and physically abused by babysitters who stayed at my house for a week while my parents went on vacation. After spending over six months trying to convince myself I was abused by babysitters, I told the truth.

Dorothy and I spent years trying to help me accept what happened to me and the impact my childhood abuse had on my ability to connect with others. We spent hours in session trying to help me develop coping strategies as my fragmented, horrific childhood began making more sense. We worked on helping me speak about my past without reliving the traumas. We talked at length about what I was feeling in my body and what my body was trying to tell me about what I was feeling. I learned how to replace shame and rage with self-love and self-compassion. I spent years grieving for all that was lost during my childhood. Gradually, I began to accept my truth and let go of my defenses.

Once I was able to acknowledge that my dad abused me, I was able to think more about my present and my future. I was able to own that I wanted to be more than a therapist and a patient. I began feeling worthy and deserving of having a support system the size of an army. I could imagine myself in an intimate relationship and having children.

As I integrated years of childhood abuse memories, I noticed a shift in my private practice. I began working much more with clients who had horrific abuse histories. I began counseling more men and women who broke their silence decades after they experienced being physically, emotionally, or sexually abused and neglected in their childhoods. I began learning more about different therapeutic strategies that I could use to help support clients in their healing. I would use various parts of my healing experience to try and help clients move through the speaking and recovering process with less pain and less loss.

When I think back to that day when I told Dorothy what was done to me as a child and the years to follow, I think about all the men and women who are suffering in silence. I think about all the years I went to therapy, three to four times a week, just to keep myself safe and moving forward. When I broke my silence in 1999, topics like childhood abuse and sexual assault were hardly spoken about. Survivors were being disbelieved and resources for victims were limited.

Once the #MeToo movement came to life, many more men and women were speaking up about being sexually assaulted by men in powerful positions. However, there still was very little attention given to the millions of men and women who were abused as children by their parents, coaches, doctors, teachers, and others in positions of authority.

INTRODUCTION

Months after Judge Rosemarie Aquilina sentenced former Olympic doctor Larry Nassar to 40 to 175 years for abusing at least 160 gymnasts and athletes, I connected with her and many of Nassar's victims. Finally, the world was being shown that these types of crimes against children have devastating effects. For seven days, I watched dozens of Nassar's victims confront him in court. Many women stood before him giving their victim impact statement. Aly Raisman looked Nassar in the eye saying, "The effects of your actions are far reaching. Abuse goes way beyond the moment, often haunting survivors for the rest of their lives, making it difficult to trust and impacting their relationships."

When I listened to Raisman and other gymnasts talk about the impact of the abuse, I decided I needed to write this book![1] I knew the effects of childhood abuse had a tremendous impact on our ability to trust ourselves and others. I knew that the years of undigested feelings and memories were wreaking havoc on our functioning on many levels. I had experienced and witnessed dozens of clients who were barely keeping themselves alive as they began to speak up about what was done to them by their parents, or other family members or trusted authority figures. On many occasions I was told "Just get over it" or "Why can't you just leave that in the past," when I tried to get support during my recovery. I had spoken to several clients who also were invalidated and banished from their families for telling the truth.

Most of the clients I have worked with in my private practice did not tell me about what happened to them until we had been in therapy for at least two years. In fact, most of my clients did not know that what was done to them was abuse until they became parents themselves or had been adults for years and understood what happened to them. For example, I have counseled dozens of people who were emotionally and physically abused by family members or others close to their families. Most of the clients who sought out treatment with me did not start dealing with their childhood traumas until they were in their thirties, forties, and even sixties. I met one male client who just started talking about the abandonment by his father and emotional neglect by his mother after battling with major depressive disorder until his late sixties. I met another female client who did not realize that growing up in a family filled with domestic violence was what kept her stuck in an abusive marriage for over twenty-five years.

I wanted to write this book for all the people in this world who have gone unnoticed and who struggle with demons and traumas from their childhood. I want you to feel differently about your healing process when you finish this book. I want you to understand the impact of your experience. I want you to be able to identify a host of strategies that you can implement in your healing. I want you to understand the impact your abuse has had on you and how you can flip horror, shame, and grief into hope, victory, and peace. I want you to be able to share your thoughts with loved ones or people that support you so they can be better equipped to give you what you need. I want you to find your voice and figure out how you can use your pain to change your life moving forward. I want you to be able to sit in your body without feeling shame or rage.

I wanted to write this book so I could offer insights I did not have early in my healing and to serve as a guide for you in your journey. I wanted to incorporate all the lessons I have learned as a patient and a therapist. I want you to feel less alone and know that whatever you are feeling is normal, after surviving something that is not normal. I want you to be able to honor and heal your body. I want you to be able to sit in your body and to trust your gut. I want you to understand the pathology of your perpetrators or dysfunctional family system, and I want you to stop blaming yourselves for the choices others made when you were a child.

If it works for you, grab a notebook or a journal and write down statements or questions you want to continue exploring in your healing. Think about what you want in your life moving forward and know that anything is possible, if you believe it can be so. It is important to move ahead with caution and give yourself the time and space you need to process and digest what you read in the chapters ahead. Take breaks. Talk to others. Reach out to your therapist. Journal your thoughts and feelings.

One of the biggest lessons I have learned in this crazy-making process as a survivor and therapist is that we need to learn how to set boundaries and replace self-destruction with self-care. We need to check in with ourselves, identify what we are feeling, and make appropriate choices at the time. We need to be able to place our feelings when we are triggered and have a host of coping strategies when the flashbacks, nightmares, or feelings take hold of our minds and bodies. We need to recognize that we cannot cure our PTSD. We cannot make our past disappear. We can learn how to live with and accept our truth. We need to find ways to stop our childhood abuse from coming into our present. We need to figure out how to train our minds to stay in the moment versus live like we are in a constant state of danger. And we can do that with tons of support and self-care. We have choices. We are not just survivors of childhood abuse. We are parents, partners, and friends; and there are people in this world that need us to be okay! I hope by the end of this book you feel empowered, validated, heard, and understood. I hope you learn how to love and nurture your younger self and that any remnants of shame or despair fade back into your past!

Note to Readers: All identities have been changed and disguised to protect my clients' privacy.

Forms of Childhood Abuse

APPROXIMATELY ONE IN FOUR CHILDREN EXPERIENCE SOME TYPE of child abuse or neglect in their lifetime. According to the CDC, 750 children died in 2020 from abuse or neglect.[1] Government officials warn these numbers are likely an underestimate because many cases go unreported. According to the National Library of Medicine, one out of three girls and one out of five boys will be sexually abused before they reach age eighteen.[2] Ninety percent of child sexual abuse victims are abused by a family member or someone they know. Rates of child abuse are five times higher for children in families with low socioeconomic status. Over 3 million cases of child abuse and neglect are reported every year.

Child abuse and neglect are serious public health problems that need much more attention. Neglect is the most common form of child abuse that is reported. These cases make up more than 60 percent of abuse cases. Children experience these types of abuse by parents, caregivers, teachers, coaches, doctors, and religious leaders.

Physical Abuse

Physical child abuse occurs when a child is purposely physically injured or put at risk of harm by another person. Examples include hitting, kicking, shaking, burning, or other forms of force against a child. When parents choose to use physical punishment as a form of discipline, that is still considered physical abuse. Signs to look out for are unexplained bruises, broken bones, or fractures or burns. Children often don't have an explanation that matches the harm inflicted when an adult asks them why and where those injuries occur. In most cases children feel guilty, ashamed, and confused, and they are afraid to tell anyone about the abuse. There are usually red flags when a child is being harmed physically. These warning signs include withdrawal or isolation from their friends, changes in behavior, changes in school performance, depression, anxiety, panic, loss of self-confidence, sleep disruption, nightmares, and frequent absences from school or extracurricular sports. Teenagers who are being abused may exude rebellious or defiant behavior, self-harm, and even suicide attempts.

Risk factors in younger children include colicky babies, toilet-training accidents, poverty, and addiction or untreated mental health problems with one or both parents and caregivers. Other factors that put children at higher risk are when parents are engaged in criminal activity or there is domestic violence between adults living in the home. Large family size or parents who act like having children is a problem are also indicative in many cases of child physical abuse. Keep in mind, there are children who are physically abused who do not have high risk factors in their home environment. No child is immune from having harm inflicted upon them by a trusted adult or authority figure.

Sexual Abuse

Child sexual abuse is any sexual activity with a minor under eighteen years old. Different types of sexual contact, such as sexual touching, oral-genital contact, or intercourse are forms of abuse. Child sexual abuse can also involve noncontact activities, such as forcing children to watch pornography or witnessing an adult acting out sexually. Other forms of abuse are sexual harassment, prostitution, and sex trafficking. Warning signs that a child may be a victim are pregnancy, sexually transmitted infections, genital or anal pain, bleeding, or inappropriate sexual behavior with other children.

Child sexual abuse does not discriminate; however, there are factors that can make some children more susceptible to this type of abuse. Children between the ages of seven and thirteen are at highest risk. Children who live in homes with one parent or a parent and his or her partner increase the likelihood of sexual abuse. Females are five times more likely to be abused. Twenty percent of these children are abused by the age of eight. The risk is three times higher for children whose parents are not working. Predators tend to look for children who are passive, quiet, troubled, lonely, insecure, or overly trusting.[3]

There are several indicators that a child is being sexually abused. Some behaviors to keep an eye out for are excessive talking about sexual topics, talking very little to others, not wanting to be left alone with certain caretakers, or being afraid of separating from primary caregivers. Other behaviors that are indicative of child sexual abuse are bedwetting, thumb sucking, being overly compliant, spending excessive amounts of time alone, and trying to avoid bathing or changing clothes.

Emotional signs that a child is being sexually abused are a change in eating patterns, change in mood or personality, decrease in self-confidence, excessive fear, unexplained somatic complaints, such as stomach aches and headaches, a loss of interest in spending time with peers, and self-harming behaviors. The most important thing to keep in mind when there is suspicion of abuse are sudden changes in a child's behavior. If you sense in your gut something is wrong, do not avoid these feelings. Talk to other trusting adults and consider making a report to the local police or child welfare department. It is better to be wrong than turn your back on a child who may be in danger emotionally or physically.

Adults may exude signs that they are engaging in inappropriate sexual behavior with a child. Some things to watch for are adults who do not respect boundaries or listen when someone tells them "no." If an adult is engaging in conversations that are not age-appropriate, or if he or she is talking about his or her personal problems with a child, that is a warning sign of potential perpetrator behavior. If an adult is giving a child gifts without a reason or spending abundant amounts of time with a child, that indicates that the relationship is not within the adult/child boundaries.

Emotional Abuse

Emotional abuse refers to behaviors that harm a child's self-esteem or well-being. Examples include name-calling, withholding love, shaming, rejecting, or threatening harm. Risk factors include social isolation, separation from extended family, adults with a physical or mental illness, such as post-traumatic stress disorder (PTSD), eating disorders, depression, alcohol or drug dependency, financial stress, and poverty. Indicators that children exhibit when they are being emotionally abused are a lack of confidence, inability to manage their emotions, and difficulty making connections. Adults who act out emotionally onto children tend to be very judgmental, ignore boundaries, are controlling, manipulative, and dismissive of other people's feelings.

Narcissistic parental abuse is a common form of emotional abuse that is misunderstood and dismissed by many. Parents who act out in this way have an excessive need for admiration or attention at the expense of their children's well-being or regard. Some of these adults may have narcissistic personality disorder, but that is not always the case. Some adults only act in these ways toward children. In a recent article published in *Psychology Today*, Dr. Iml Lo describes three types of *parental narcissistic abuse*.[4] The first type is when parents use their children to fill their own ego. They take praise and accomplishments of their children and make it about themselves. If these children lose a game or suffer some type of setback, these adults may withdraw their love and approval. Children coming from this type of family environment often describe feeling like they are treated as a trophy versus a person. In this type of narcissistic abuse, it is common for parents to make one child the perfect one and make other children in the family the scapegoat. This type of abuse leaves the "perfect" child feeling guilty and the other siblings feeling like they are being banished.

Vulnerable narcissists are insecure and emotionally unstable. This type of abuse involves guilt trips and control. It is difficult for others to recognize because these adults often appear insecure and passive in ways others cannot see. These parents lack self-esteem and may feel isolated from other connections. They resort to control to try and get their children to be emotionally dependent upon them, to serve as an ego booster, and to improve their self-worth. Often children in these family's report feeling like the peacemaker or caregiver and sometimes they refer to themselves as the family therapist.

The third type of narcissistic parent cannot deal with feeling overshadowed by their children. They often react with anger and jealousy when their children appear to be more successful than they are. These types of parents often attack their children or give them the silent treatment when they feel inferior or outdone by their children's successes. Children living in these types of dysfunctions often describe feeling like they are walking on eggshells. I have met several clients who describe their parents as a Jekyll and Hyde, saying, "One minute my mom loves me and then like a switch comes on and she hates me, even though I have not done anything." Over time, children growing up in these types of households will learn to keep any good news or accomplishments a secret in order to protect themselves from feeling shot down or belittled. The jealousy and competitive environment will also leave other members of the household feeling guilty for being happy or having any type of success. In some cases, these children will self-sabotage to avoid feeling guilty.

Neglect
Neglect is the failure to meet a child's needs, physically and emotionally. This may include housing, food, clothing, or access to education or medical care. Children being neglected often have poor hygiene, are inappropriately dressed for weather, have unmet medical and dental care, are unsupervised at home, and experience failure to thrive and malnutrition. Some children who are neglected will beg for food or steal, miss school, or show up unannounced at other people's homes. Some of the emotional signs that a child is being neglected are excessive willingness to please, parentified and acting like adults, on edge most of the time, or has learning issues but no specific educational deficit. These children may act out at school, have very low self-esteem, or be emotionally detached. Over 59 percent of all reported cases of child abuse constitute neglect.

LONG-TERM EFFECTS OF CHILDHOOD ABUSE
The effects of long-term childhood abuse can be devastating and life-altering years into one's adulthood. There are physical, psychological, and behavioral problems adult survivors grapple with. Even years, or decades after the mistreatment ends, survivors may find themselves dealing with mental disorders, somatic issues, and other health problems. The impact often runs throughout a family system for multiple generations, which causes some survivors to repeat the abuse done to them onto their spouses or children. Some of the health problems reported by survivors include high blood pressure, chronic pain, cancer, gastrointestinal problems, diabetes, and heart and lung disease. Some survivors are also at risk for stunted brain development. According to researchers at the BetterHelp therapy platform, regions of the brain, including the amygdala and the hippocampus, can be negatively affected by all types of abuse.[5] These parts of the brain process emotions and the hippocampus is critical for retaining information.

According to the National Institute of Justice, children who are neglected or abused are more likely to develop antisocial behaviors or may associate with others who have antisocial tendencies. This study also concluded that males are more likely to display bullying and aggression, while females tend to struggle with high levels of anxiety or be socially withdrawn.[6]

Experiencing any type of child abuse or neglect as a young child is also a risk factor for developing different types of psychiatric disorders as adults, including depression, anxiety, PTSD, eating disorders, and behavioral disorders. Research has also found that childhood trauma and the effects on the brain leave these children more vulnerable to developing psychiatric issues. While experiencing child abuse and neglect increases your chances of struggling with these issues, no study has found that all adults are destined to deal with any type of psychiatric condition lifelong.

The disruption of brain development can impact executive function skills, such as memory, self-awareness, planning, and problem solving. These issues often result in learning disabilities, poor grades, and a higher chance of dropping out of school. Many studies have been conducted on the correlation between surviving childhood abuse and developing attention deficit hyperactivity disorder (ADHD). According to the National Child Traumatic Stress Network, researchers disagree on whether ADHD is associated with childhood abuse and neglect. Some pediatric studies conclude that youth with ADHD are more likely than those without ADHD to develop child traumatic stress. Other studies indicate that children who are abused are at higher risk of developing ADHD.[7]

Young children who are abused or neglected may exhibit symptoms of hyperactivity and disruptive behavior that resembles ADHD disorder. Children who are living in abusive environments often appear to be agitated, nervous, and on high alert. These behaviors can be mistaken for symptoms of ADHD. Some children who are unable to focus or pay attention may be displaying symptoms of dissociation versus attention problems.

During the last twenty-seven years, I have counseled clients who have reported all the above long-term effects of childhood abuse. I have met clients who suffer from chronic pain, severe depression, colitis, heart problems, addictions, high blood pressure, migraines, ADHD, and of course PTSD. Part of the challenge in the healing process is trying to identify which came first. For example, I am working with one client named Elissa who often questions her ADHD diagnosis. We have talked extensively about her dissociative tendencies and how they look very similar to what doctors have referred to as ADHD. I work with another female client in her thirties, who has struggled with chronic neck and back pain beginning in her adolescence. Throughout treatment she has spoken about the link between holding anger and sadness in her body after her father abandoned her and her mother when she was seven years old. There were many times in therapy when I questioned my severe depression diagnosis. I often wondered and still question if I would have had a history of suicide attempts and severe depression if I was not abused by my father? While there is no way to know which came first, many survivors want to know what caused their psychosomatic or psychiatric disorders.

What Is C-PTSD?

Complex post-traumatic stress disorder, or C-PTSD, is a type of post-traumatic caused by extensive, long-lasting, or repeated acts of trauma. Most survivors of childhood abuse develop symptoms of C-PTSD as they become adults. Most forms of PTSD are caused by a single event, such as a car accident, a sexual assault, or an isolated incidence of child physical or sexual abuse. The DSM-5 currently does not distinguish between PTSD and C-PTSD as separate conditions. There have been at least twenty-nine studies that support the validity of using a separate diagnosis for complex PTSD, and it is now an official diagnosis in the ICD-11.[8]

The effects of ongoing childhood abuse caused by parents or caregivers change the brain and also change us at a core level. It changes the way we view the world and how we view others. There are a variety of symptoms we experience as survivors of complex trauma. Throughout the remainder of this book, I will share coping strategies and ways to work through and manage symptoms of C-PTSD.

People who suffer abuse by significant people in their lives develop an intense fear of trusting people. It takes very little for us to become distrusting of anyone in the role of authority. If the brain senses danger, any trust built will be destroyed. Deep fears of trust lead to extreme aloneness. Many clients have described feeling like they are living in this world alone, even when they have partners, friends, or loved ones who feel love and support for them. I have had hundreds of conversations with my therapist about the isolation I have felt during my abuse and for years to follow. Repeatedly, I told Dorothy, "I feel like I do not fit in anywhere. I do not trust anyone." I would often find reasons not to trust Dorothy, even when she did nothing wrong. If she had the slightest change in her facial expressions or seemed disinterested, I would tell her she only listened to me because I paid her money. Those kinds of statements have been said to me by my clients as well.

Other symptoms of C-PTSD involve difficulty in regulating our emotions. We may have intense reactions in situations where the feelings do not match the present. For example, one of my male clients, who was physically abused by his father and sexually abused by his priest, found himself losing his temper at the most insignificant circumstances. If someone cut him off while he was driving or his wife told him she needed something, he would fly off the handle. He found himself cursing and throwing objects in his car and in his house when he could not manage his emotions.

He broke several devices and his wife threatened to divorce him if he did not learn how to manage his anger.

Most childhood abuse survivors with C-PTSD report having a variety of flashbacks. Visual flashbacks are when the mind is triggered, and you feel like you are reliving the abuse in the present. Somatic flashbacks, which I have referred to as body memories, are when we feel sensations, pain, and discomfort in parts of our bodies that were harmed. Usually, these feelings are triggered by memories or feelings about something we are struggling with in the present. For example, when I felt angry with Dorothy or someone close to me, I would feel like my private parts were being violated. I worked with another young female in her twenties, who would report waking up in the morning feeling like her arms and feet were restrained during the night. When she was having memories, her body would reexperience what she felt when her uncle was sexually abusing her in her sleep. Emotional flashbacks are the least understood, and at times, can feel crazy-making. Many clients have described feeling the remnants of shame, fear, and anger when they were trying to connect with their partners, children, or loved ones. I have referred to these types of flashbacks as "feeling" flashbacks. The male client I mentioned above often felt deep pain and shame in the present when he had to confront coworkers. During one of our sessions, he had an emotional flashback during the session as he talked about what happened with his coworker. He told me, "I feel like I am ten-years old again and that I am about to lose everything because I spoke up." He had explained that his coworker became defensive and threatening as he told his colleague what he had done wrong. I could feel him shrinking up on the sofa as he talked about this experience. We were able to identify that he was having an emotional flashback of feeling shame and fear after he told an adult he was being abused by his priest. Oftentimes, emotional flashbacks are hard to identify at the moment. Part of the healing process is about identifying when old feelings are creeping into present day experiences.

When we are triggered by circumstances in the present, it takes hard work and dedication to get in touch with the part of us that is shifting into the past emotionally.

Another commonly reported symptom of C-PTSD is hypervigilance. If someone shows the slightest change in his or her body language, tone of voice, or facial expression, it will immediately send us into pending doom and danger. Many C-PTSD survivors report a loss in their faith, whether it is about people, the world, religion, or even a loss of faith about self. I have met dozens of men and women who were abused by religious leaders. Most of them have told me they would never step foot back into a church or synagogue. Reclaiming faith is attainable when we realize that not all religious leaders are pedophiles or abusers.

Childhood complex trauma survivors often have a wounded inner child that continues to affect them in adulthood. When a child's emotional needs are neglected or when a child is repeatedly physically or sexually abused, this deeply affects their emotional development. I have never met a client who has not described feeling like their younger selves have been damaged or ruined. For years I searched for adults who could give me what I needed from my parents. I began looking for love and nurturance from teachers, coaches, and family friends during elementary school. At the time I did not know I was trying to fill a void that was missing in my family. I did not know until years into my healing that I was longing for a mother and father figure. Recently, one of my clients talked to me about craving love from a woman. She experienced transference with me, which meant that she wanted me to be the mother she never had. Throughout the book I will share more about how to heal our hurt inner child and no longer allow those feelings to interfere in relationships in the present.

Most survivors with C-PTSD report feeling an ongoing feeling of hopelessness or shame. The extensive abuse or neglect history leaves most of us feeling like things will never be okay. We became used to living in an environment that felt unsafe and harmful, and most of us felt like no one would ever help us. These feelings continue long into adulthood because that is what we expect to happen over and over again. Reclaiming life in adulthood requires us to access the part of ourselves that has choices and a voice. Learning how to manage shame and be open to hope is possible. Making space for hope does not mean that we need a rescuer or someone that can make all of our pain go away. When we feel helpless, we can do things that make us feel hopeful. When survivors continue looking for rescuers, they attract the wrong types of people and end up being retraumatized repeatedly. For example, I have counseled dozens of clients who have been in numerous abusive and toxic relationships in adulthood, hoping for the same outcome of being saved by someone else. Breaking the cycle of toxic relationships means being able to make choices to set boundaries or walk away from people who re-create memories from our abusive past.

One of the most detrimental effects of chronic childhood abuse is that it puts survivors at high risk for suicidal thoughts, suicide ideation, or being actively suicidal. Suicide ideation becomes a way of coping. It is a way out in a situation where there is no way out. The deep pain that comes from knowing and speaking up about childhood abuse also can be unbearable, especially in the beginning of the healing journey. Finding ways to manage and understand where these feelings come from is crucial for survivors. Most of my clients have reported a history of suicide attempts and suicidal ideation. I worked with one woman in her forties who was hospitalized over ten times in her twenties, after multiple suicide attempts and self-harming behaviors. Years into her healing, she realized that she wanted to stop living because she did not want to accept the sexual abuse done to her by her father and her priest. She also learned that her suicidal thoughts were also emotional flashbacks from her childhood. She reported many times during her childhood when she considered suicide because "no one cared about me, and I was trapped."

Actionable Steps We Can Take to Heal from C-PTSD

1. *Create safety and a sense of security.* Form an army of people that can support you in your physical, mental, and emotional well-being.

2. *Find a good trauma therapist!* Jump to chapter 3 to learn more about finding a therapist that is trauma informed and understands the impact of childhood abuse.

3. *Practice remembering and mourning each time a new memory breaks through.* We cannot recover without acknowledging the truth and giving ourselves opportunities to grieve for all that was lost during our childhood.

4. *When you want to avoid your feelings, think about the benefits of facing them!* We needed to shut down and numb ourselves during the abuse. But now we can sit with our feelings because we are adults and we have choices about who we tell, how we react, and what we do with the information that has broken into our consciousness.

5. *Keep your notebook at hand* so you can explore different types of therapeutic strategies, such as EMDR (eye movement desensitization and reprocessing), to help you move through the remembering process.

6. *If the remembering process makes you feel unsafe, go back to step one.* Create safety. Take a break from the trauma work. Revisit your support network and implement new strategies if the ones you have been using are not supporting you in staying stable and present.

7. *Healing from C-PTSD takes time, and it is a process.* Integrating memories and finding ways to stay present in your body and mind is the goal. Every time you work through another part of your abusive past, you are taking steps to reconnect with yourself and find connection with others.

8. *You are not alone.* Take as many people as you need throughout parts of your journey as you work toward reclaiming your life in adulthood!

Chapter 2

Remembering Your Abuse

"I have risked everything to tell the truth. Tell the truth."
—Maya Angelou

Breaking the Silence

From early childhood, many of us learned to be silent. Some of us grew up with messages that led us to believe that "children should be seen and not heard." Most adults assumed that if we said nothing, that all was good. Up until a few years ago, most of society had turned a blind eye to children who may have been in physical or emotional danger.

Talking about childhood abuse has been a taboo topic for most of my twenty-five-plus-year career as a therapist. Social media did not exist until the last ten years. Up until a few years ago, there were very few online resources or hotlines people could call if they were in danger or if they knew a child who may be in an unsafe relationship with an adult.

The Child Abuse Prevention and Treatment Act (CAPTA), passed by the federal government in 1974 and reauthorized in 2010, is the largest body of legislation regarding the fair, ethical, and legal treatment of children and is intended to keep them free from all forms of abuse including physical, sexual, emotional, and psychological.[1] There are mandatory reporting laws that require professionals in the healthcare field or those working closely with children to report any suspected case of childhood abuse or neglect to the police or child protective services.

While there have been laws set in place for over fifty years, many cases of child abuse go unreported. The risk of breaking up a family or turning in an authority figure is no less intimidating now than it was in the 1970s. Sadly, most people are unable to break the silence about their abuse until years after it ended, and they have become financially independent adults.

There are several reasons why children are unable to speak up about abuse over the time period it occurs. Often, abusive adults convince their children that they won't be believed, or if they speak up they will be punished. Most children care about their abusers, and they feel it is their responsibility to protect the ones that are causing them harm. In most cases, there are enablers or other adults who collude with the abusers. If children speak, they risk losing relationships with all of those involved. Abuse does not happen every day. Many children who have been neglected, beaten, or violated sexually also have received gifts and had positive experiences with the same adults who have hurt or neglected them. Furthermore, children tend to blame themselves for everything that happens to them. Many clients have shared with me that at the time of their abuse they felt like they had caused their abuser to hurt them. They have said things to me like, "If only I had been better at school," "if only I did not spend their money," or "if only I was less friendly." Children rationalize the pathology of their abusers and make it all their fault. In most cases, children have no idea that what is being done to them is wrong or unacceptable. Here are some of the reasons why children don't break the silence as children.

- They promised to keep the abuse secret.

- They have been given gifts to keep it a secret.
- They have been threatened by the offender to not speak.
- They feel guilty because they believe that the abuse is their fault.
- They are ashamed to tell.
- They are confused because the abuser is someone they know and trust.
- They have been convinced that the abuse is normal or okay.
- They are too young to know that the abuse isn't appropriate—especially if it's done by someone they know and trust.
- They have not been taught that abuse is not okay.
- They don't have the words to use to tell.
- They don't want to lose their house or their family.
- They don't want to get someone in trouble.

At the beginning of 2019, child abuse received more media attention with the release of *Abducted in Plain Sight*, *Surviving R. Kelly*, and *Leaving Neverland*. These documentaries received an outpouring of support and millions of viewers began speaking out against their abusers on social media. A year before these documentaries were released, the world was captivated by the conviction of Olympic doctor Larry Nassar. On December 16, 2016, Nassar was arrested after the FBI had found more than thirty-seven thousand images of child pornography and a video of Nassar allegedly molesting underage girls. He was denied bail and ordered to remain in federal prison. On April 6, 2017, his medical license was revoked for three years. The former doctor for the American gymnastics team was sentenced to 40 to 175 years in prison on January 18, 2018, for multiple sex crimes, capping an extraordinary seven-day hearing that drew more than 150 young women to publicly confront him and speak of their abuse.[2]

The dramatic increase of media coverage on stories related to childhood abuse has created more social awareness, and it also has forced the public to recognize the magnitude of these types of traumas. While most people do not want to believe that one person is capable of harming hundreds of children, the case against Nassar proved to the world that it is possible. For seven days, the public listened to 159 alleged accusers confront Nassar as they shared their victim impact statement. Nassar's abuse and sentencing helped change public attitudes about childhood abuse, starting with the importance of believing victims when they report their experiences. After Nassar's sentencing, millions of men and women took to social media sharing their harrowing stories of surviving different types of childhood abuse. High profile cases of alleged childhood abuse have encouraged more adults who were abused as children to come forward and speak up about what happened to them.

While social media has contributed to an increase in adults sharing their stories of abuse as children, there are many other factors and transitions in life that lead people to open years of buried memories and secrets. I spent years trying to keep my memories of abuse hidden from my awareness. I wanted my life to be normal, and I did not want to risk losing my relationships with my family. I wanted to be a "good" daughter, and I felt like it was my job to protect everyone around me. Before I started therapy in my mid-twenties, there were many times when the memories and words were on the tip of my tongue, but then my unconscious defense mechanisms kicked in and I went back into denial. At the time, I did not know that I was having flashbacks or that I had been dissociating. I just rationalized these feelings by convincing myself that I had done something that caused my body to feel pain or anguish.

After spending over two years in weekly therapy, I began feeling frustrated and hopeless about my life and my future. I started thinking more about family and relationships, and I was tired of living an incomplete life. I wanted to do more than counsel clients in therapy. I wanted to have deeper connections and I wanted to embrace my body rather than hate it. At that time the guilt and fear consumed me, and these feelings stopped me from breaking my silence about my history of childhood abuse.

Many clients have told me that they cannot dive into their abusive past, saying things like, "I could lose my family if I speak," or "It will change how I feel toward my family or the people that were supposed to protect me."

Most of my clients who have a history of abuse have told me that they felt like they lost years of their lives in their adulthood, trying to sweep earlier traumatic memories under the rug. I worked with one man in his fifties, whom I will call Gary, who told me he lost his marriage because of a horrific past. Gary started working with me in therapy a year after his wife divorced him. He shared with me that their relationship disintegrated because of his explosive episodes. Gary assumed that his anger was tied to stressors at work. He lacked awareness about where his rage was coming from. Gary grew up in a single parent household, with a mother who was physically and emotionally abusive. When we started therapy Gary did not talk about what it was like to feel neglected, deprived, or ashamed when his mother beat him. In fact, he was unable to talk about his abuse until over a year into our relationship.

One day he walked into my office and he told me, "I cannot do this anymore." He began talking about his previous marriage and how he felt triggered when he thought his ex-wife was mad at him. Gary started opening up about their relationship and how inadequate he felt as a husband. He shared with me that he said the same things to his ex-wife that his mother said to him when she was mad at him. Gary told me that he had no right to be married and that he would never date again.

As time went on, Gary started to feel differently about relationships. He started noticing his sexual feelings and interest in women. He wanted to allow himself the opportunity to explore dating in his fifties. A part of him knew that if he wanted to have a life moving forward, he would need to talk more about what happened to him as a child and the impact that had on his ability to connect with women as an adult. During one session Gary described an incident that sounded to me like physical abuse. He told me about a beating that left him bruised and full of shame. Gary found ways to excuse his mother's behavior, mostly by blaming himself. For Gary, the first step to breaking the silence meant acknowledging that he was abused by his mother. It took Gary several more sessions of processing his earlier memories to come to terms with what his mother had done to him. He recounted several incidents from when he was married, and he felt like his body was consumed with rage. Once Gary was able to recognize that he was repeating behaviors onto his ex-wife that were done to him by his mother, he began his healing journey.

It can take years for survivors to recognize what happened to them was some form of child abuse. Research studies indicate that more than half of adults who were abused as children are repressing the trauma. Therapists have found that abuse experienced early in life can overwhelm the central nervous system, causing children to split off a painful memory from their conscious awareness. A study published in the *American Journal of Psychiatry*, highlights the findings that many adults who were abused as children dissociated and repressed their memories. "They maintain that this psychological defense mechanism—known as dissociative amnesia—turns up routinely in patients they encounter." Repressed memories are memories that we unconsciously avoid thinking about, usually because the experiences left us feeling traumatized.

People can unconsciously block any memories associated with their abuse for years.[3]

Monumental life events such as a wedding, birth of a child, or the death of a parent or immediate family member can trigger the memories to become conscious. Blocking memories into our unconscious serves as a defense mechanism. No one chooses to repress or forget what happened to us. In fact, many survivors I have met have told me that forgetting what they experienced or what was done to them in childhood protected them from going insane. Our survival mechanisms kick in from a very early age. When children sense danger, they fight back in silence. Repressed memories, also referred to as dissociative amnesia, are common in people who have experienced adverse childhood experiences. Physical abuse, sexual abuse, emotional neglect, and emotional abuse are forms of traumas that can lead to repressed memories. Some of us block out small portions of time, while others are unable to recall years of their childhood. These memories are thought to be unconsciously blocked for several years and are recovered later, often from a trigger.

Repressing our earlier traumas during adulthood can only work for so long. The more we try to push these negative thoughts and feelings out of our mind, the more we experience flashbacks, nightmares, and psychosomatic symptoms. For example, I have met several clients who have a history of migraines, back pain, gastrointestinal problems, and excessive feelings of guilt. Some of the men and women I have counseled who were repressing their abuse also struggled with intimacy, and many had avoided having partners or starting families to keep their memories buried in their unconscious. Most of my clients who were repressed also reported having low self-esteem, trust issues, codependent relationships, mood swings, hypervigilance, inability to focus, and avoidant behaviors.

Not all survivors of childhood abuse completely forget or repress what happened to them. About half of the clients I have seen in therapy have some recollection of things that were done to them or experiences gone through growing up. For example, I worked with one male in his fifties, whom I will refer to as Mark, who was able to tell me from the onset of our relationship that he was physically abused by his father. During our third session he told me about an incident when his dad "beat the crap out of me," after he accidentally broke a window while playing ball in his yard. Mark was able to identify that he had been physically abused as a child, and he was able to tell me about ten other incidents involving his father, but the facts surrounding his abuse were fragmented and out of sequence.

It took Mark years of being in therapy to acknowledge that his father abused him. Mark spent most of his life denying the severity of his abuse, and instead he blamed himself for what his father had done to him. It was not until after his father passed away that he broke his silence. He came to session one week, sat on my sofa, and just burst into tears. He told me about a confrontation he'd had with his boss at the time. Mark recognized that he went into fight or flight whenever he needed to ask someone in authority for help or he needed to set a boundary. Mark told me, "Every time I need to set a limit or ask an authority for something that I need, I picture that person beating up on me." He went on to describe his frustration with constantly being afraid of getting in trouble. For Mark, this was the beginning of his healing journey to be able to identify that he was physically abused by his father.

It takes a long time for survivors to acknowledge they were mistreated or neglected by people who were supposed to care for them. Oftentimes, many of us were not able to make the connection between the struggles we have had in our lives and how that is connected to what happened to us as children. The longer we fight the truth, the more disrupted our lives become in the present. Breaking the silence is a process that happens over time.

Actionable Steps You Can Take after You Break Your Silence
1. Begin setting up support for yourself. If you feel comfortable, reach out to a friend or partner or someone you trust and let them know you are beginning to speak up about what happened to you during your childhood.

2. Buy a notebook or journal so you can write down what you remember.

3. Do not expect yourself to speak about your past in one session or in one conversation. When you find the words to your experience, give yourself permission to move as slowly as you need to. If you need time to sit with your revelations or memories, that is okay!

4. Ask yourself, "Why am I choosing to speak now?" There are people who will make insensitive comments like, "Why didn't you say something sooner," or "Why did it take you so long to tell me that?" Try not to let those kinds of statements shut you down or make you feel guilty for speaking. There are some people who do not understand trauma, and there are other people who may be triggered by what you are remembering.

5. Be extra cautious and kind to yourself when you begin speaking. Think about different forms of self-care and what advice you would give to someone else going through something similar.

6. It is normal to feel overwhelmed and consumed with grief when you speak up about what happened to you. Consider talking with a therapist and/or finding a support group to help you manage all your feelings.

7. If you feel like no one will believe what you are telling them, ask yourself if you would disbelieve someone else speaking his or her truth.

8. It may have taken you years or even decades to break your silence. You would not remember these types of traumas if you were in a place in your life when you could not handle it. As you allow yourself to know what you know and feel what you feel, you are opening the door to living a much fuller life.

9. You are taking important steps to reclaim your life and feeling in charge of your choices moving forward!

10. Remember that it is not the speaking up that is the problem, it is that it happened to you, that is the problem!

MANAGING FLASHBACKS

Memories of abuse are unbearable at times, overwhelming, and unbelievable. In order to survive during the abuse, we needed to distance ourselves and turn off our reactions as it happened. Flashbacks can be worse than the actual trauma because we never know when they will end or start again.

Survivors spend years of their lives trying to protect themselves from flashbacks. Flashbacks are powerful memories that feel very real, like they are happening in the moment. Sounds, scents, or pain can all be experienced at one time. Flashbacks can make people feel "crazy" and that their life is out of control. Depending on what is happening in the moment, people can have multiple flashbacks at once. A flashback can occur at any moment, when we are awake or asleep. They can be distressing, confusing, and fragmented. Part of the goal when working with a therapist is to help us observe our emotions and what we are feeling in our bodies during the flashback.

When the memories of my abuse started to surface in my late twenties, I noticed that the flashbacks were coming back in the form of body memories. Weeks before I broke my silence, I felt like my body was being assaulted when I tried to go to sleep and when I tried to connect with anyone that had authority. Initially, I did not tell Dorothy I was having flashbacks. When we sat together in session, I just smiled and acted like everything was okay. When I felt memories of my abuse in my body, I came up with reasons why I was feeling those sensations. I convinced myself I caused harm to my body as a child instead of identifying that those feelings in my body were flashbacks.

After I opened up to Dorothy about my abuse, the flashbacks intensified. During the first several months of uncovering memories of sexual abuse, I continued to see my parents. One time when they visited me at my apartment, I went into a panic when I noticed my father's footsteps outside my bedroom door. On other occasions when I had contact with my parents, I felt like I was being raped. I had flashbacks of the penetration and other forms of abuse that were done to me by my father. I felt multiple sensations at once in my body. I was triggered by the smell of alcohol. I had body memories of injections going into my arm. I had sensory memories of what his breath smelled like and how my mouth tasted after being orally assaulted. When I went to the bathroom, I felt burning when I urinated.

I had hundreds of what I called the "day after" flashbacks. These were memories that I had the day after I was abused. I remembered being at a football game during high school and how I felt pain in my body when I walked through the stadium. I remembered waking up the next morning and feeling the physical aftermath of the assaults. I remembered staring in the mirror, trying to figure out why my body felt pain. I remembered taking evidence that I saw in my under garments and trying to hide them by throwing them in the trash. Over time I learned that these memories were coming back to help me understand how I blocked the actual abuse and also how my mind stored the memory so that eventually I could speak about the abuse.

Recently I began counseling a young woman whom I will refer to as Elissa. She started therapy after battling with a raging eating disorder and obsessive-compulsive tendencies. When I met Elissa, she was in a toxic relationship with her boyfriend. She was also being sexually and emotionally harassed by her boss at work. When I met Elissa, I had no idea that she was also struggling with PTSD. She did not report episodes of dissociation, nightmares, or suicidal tendencies. In the beginning of our relationship, we spoke mostly about her job and how to handle issues with her boss. As time went on, Elissa began losing weight, and she appeared to be more anxious and depressed. She felt unsafe in her job, and she was afraid to break up with her boyfriend. After a few months of working together in therapy, I started noticing what seemed like dissociative tendencies. Elissa struggled to make eye contact, and at times it felt like we were in two different rooms. Her affect was flat and distant. As we got to know each other better, I asked Elissa more about her childhood. With hesitation and ambivalence, Elissa slowly started divulging more about her past. She told me about an incident when she was ten years old when she saw her father choke her mother. We talked about that event and other times when she witnessed her father abusing her mother.

Once Elissa started talking more about her childhood, she started telling me about times when she felt like she could not stay in her body. She talked more about her relationship with her boyfriend and how she was triggered when he wanted to have any type of physical contact. At the time, Elissa did not know that she was having flashbacks. When Elissa wanted to say no or she wanted to quit her job, she told me she had flashes of her father putting his hands around her neck. She did not understand why these flashbacks crept in when she was at work or with her boyfriend.

One of the most important things to remember about flashbacks is that they usually intrude in the present because we are trying to process or understand the impact of earlier trauma. Elissa had a history of feeling trapped and unprotected. As she got older and she had more independence, she started realizing how much her past was affecting her present. Elissa and I talked at length about her childhood and what it was like to witness her father abuse her mother. She started writing down her flashbacks and how she was reliving her trauma in her present. She began to understand why she was attracted to men in her personal and professional life that abused her physically, sexually, and emotionally. While flashbacks are dreadful and scary, they are also presenting themselves to help us gain awareness about the repetition of earlier traumatic events. For real change to take place, we need to know how our bodies stored our abuse and how we can use that information to make healthier, safer connections in the present. There is no way to predict when or how often flashbacks will emerge. Rather than fight these memories, there are steps we can take to manage the flashbacks and continue moving forward in our healing journey.

Actionable Steps You Can Take to Manage Flashbacks

- Remind yourself that what you are experiencing is a flashback or memory. Tell yourself, "I am safe now and no longer in danger."

- Go to a safe place like the beach, a park, or somewhere in nature.

- Try some breathing techniques to calm your nervous system.

- Use mindfulness strategies: smell something—an essential oil like lavender can help to calm and soothe. Taste something—what does it taste like; is it sweet or spicy? Feel something—touch some fabric or hold a warm drink. Listen—identify the sounds you can hear around you or play some music. Sight—what things can you see around you?

- Refocus your thoughts on the present and think about two or three events that you are looking forward to. Reach out to a friend or family member. Have face-to-face contact with someone that knows you are in the healing process.

- After experiencing a flashback, be kind to yourself. Redirect yourself if you start to minimize or deny that the abuse happened. When you try to undo what you already remembered, take notice of the increase in flashbacks. Consider asking yourself, "Am I getting flooded with memories because I am trying to act like it did not happen?"

Managing the Dissociation

- Talk to your therapist or a trusted friend about what you feel when you dissociate.

- Express thoughts and feelings through activities like drawing, painting, or creative writing.

- Write down the nightmare or flashback and change the ending. For example, if you remember feeling abandoned, do something that makes you feel connected and protected.

- Mindfully eat a piece of candy—think about how sweet it tastes.

- Speak kindly to yourself—"I am strong. I am brave. I can handle this. I can stay in my body now because I am safe!"

- Hold onto an ice cube, take a hot shower, smell the flowers in your backyard, walk barefoot on the grass or sand.

- Try the tapping strategy! It is a technique that allows you to feel in control of your body and stay in the present. If you feel like you are leaving your body or having a flashback, create a statement that affirms your strength and bravery. For example, say to yourself, "I can handle this," or "My brain would not let me remember this thought or feeling if I was not strong enough to face it." Say that statement to yourself while tapping on your chest, legs, or temples. Repeat this strategy at least five times. This strategy is calming and grounding, and you can do it anywhere, anytime!

- Look around you and describe the objects in the room or colors on the wall.
- Watch a funny movie and laugh out loud.
- Reorient yourself by saying the day, time, and year.
- Be patient. Acknowledge that dissociation is the defense you use to help you survive. Remind yourself that you do not need to continue leaving your body because you are safe now! Give yourself grace. You cannot just stop having flashbacks or dissociating. Recovery is a process that takes place over the course of time.

Moving Safely through Recovery

Once you have broken your silence and you recognize that you are having flashbacks, it is crucial to set up a plan that allows you to move safely through this part of the process. You spent years of your life trying to survive. Your life is too valuable for you to let this part of your healing sabotage what you have worked to accomplish up until now. Working through childhood abuse is one of the biggest challenges you may ever encounter.

Many of us have resorted to drugs, eating disorders, or other forms of behavior that numb our memories and feelings. When the memories come flooding back into our awareness, our bodies may reexperience the rage and helplessness. During our childhood we did not have the words or understand how to describe what we were living through. In order to heal, we need to revisit some of the worst times in our lives as children. The goal is not to relive or retraumatize us. Rather, we need to remember that we are on a healing journey so we can understand our past and why our bodies and minds are not always able to stay grounded and in the present.

One of the most important parts of this journey is to be able to find the words and identify our feelings, so we can begin to heal. In a study led by Bessel van der Kolk in 1991, reports suggested that many adults who engage in self-destructive behaviors have a history of childhood abuse and neglect.[4] The challenge to moving safely through our healing process is finding balance. It is important to take time to process and digest your feelings. However, it is also crucial to make space to live your life in the present.

When someone dies, in most cases we attend a funeral, and we may take off a few days from work to deal with our grief. Every time you have a new memory or you put another piece of your past together, you may need to create a ritual or give yourself time and space to work through those feelings. It is helpful to have plans lined up or know that you will be spending time focusing on something that has to do with your present as you face your past. Think about different places you can go to as you uncover and speak about memories.

There were times when I spent hours on hiking trails with my dog Chloe, after I told Dorothy about something else I had remembered from my childhood. Some of my clients focus on their hobbies or activities that help them stay in their bodies, such as singing, writing, and crafting. Moving with extreme caution, patience, and determination helps to contain the emotions and allows you to continue reclaiming life in the present. As you read through the book, there will be many more strategies and techniques and ideas you can implement on your journey.

1. Make a vision board or write a list of reasons why you are addressing your trauma now. For example, "I am doing this now because I want a partner" or "I want to feel less afraid to set boundaries with my husband and my family."

2. Make a plan for safety immediately after your therapy session ends. Make plans with a friend or return to work. If you need time to process the session before moving on with the day, grab a notebook and write down some thoughts and feelings. Remind yourself that therapy is a process and that you do not have to deal with all of your feelings in one

session or one day. Reassure yourself that you and your therapist will not forget what you have talked about in therapy and that your memories will not disappear.

3. If you are feeling worse or stranded after the therapy session ends, make sure to tell your therapist. You may need to take some time at the end of a session to shift gears and focus on something lighter—for example, talking about a show you are watching or something you are looking forward to doing before your next session.

4. Use your pets as support. Plan hikes or walks or adventures you can go on if you have a dog. Focus on the love you feel for your pets and how they need you to be safe so you can continue to love them.

5. If you are flooded with flashbacks, memories, or nightmares, think about taking a break from working through all your flashbacks. Tell yourself it is okay to pause and get back to trauma work. Talk with your therapist about how you can honor the work you have already done. Focus on your progress; for example, maybe you set a boundary with a colleague or maybe you feel more grounded when triggers are present. It is important to acknowledge all parts of this crazy-making process. Trauma work does not require you to always talk about something that happened to you in childhood.

6. Limit your time on social media. Images of gun violence, sexual assault, or war can lead to more feelings of fear and isolation. Take notice of who you follow on social media. Look for words of hope and inspiration.

7. When you feel overwhelmed or alone, imagine people who love you taking some of these feelings and holding them for you. For example, picture your therapist or your best friend or partner telling you, "You got this," or "You are worth the

fight." Sometimes knowing that others believe in us, even if they do not fully understand the journey, can make a big difference.

8. Use self-compassion when you can. Talk to your younger self that felt abandoned, afraid, or abused. Tell that younger part of you, "It was not your fault," or "You are not the cause of bad things happening to others." Write a letter to your younger self and share that in a session. Remind yourself that old feelings of inadequacy or hopelessness will not last forever. When you feel unsafe or self-destructive, do the opposite. For example, when you want to hurt yourself, take a bath, go for a hike, or sit by a warm fire. Remind yourself that urges to self-harm come and go. Voice the urge and notice that it will pass if you hold it and move on to something else.

CHAPTER 3

Therapeutic Modalities in Recovery

WHAT ARE EMDR, DBT, AND IFS?

Childhood abuse affects all areas of one's life. For most of us, the impact of our experiences shows up as we become adults. The memories imprinted in our brains and bodies affect us in our relationships, our mood, and our sense of self. There are effective treatments that will help us heal. Throughout the years I have been offering psychodynamic counseling, which stresses the importance of the unconscious and how our past experiences determine our current behavior. I decided to use this type of approach after spending years in therapy with Dorothy, examining and exploring my reactions to situations in the present. After extensive sessions, Dorothy helped me understand that my choices and relationships in the present were largely based on my traumatic past.

For example, I noticed that I was attracted to people who had narcissistic tendencies, especially in dating relationships. I also learned that I gravitated toward people who were emotionally limited. I found myself feeling dissatisfied and invisible in most of my friendships. Often I played the role of the rescuer or caretaker. I was friends with a couple of women who were having extramarital affairs. I became their secret keeper, and I thought if I could support them in getting what they wanted, I would get what I wanted. There were many times when I would talk to Dorothy about feeling uncared about with many of my friends. She explained to me that I was re-creating the longing I felt with my parents. I yearned for love and acceptance. On some level, I decided that I was not worthy of being in reciprocal relationships. I thought I had to earn my keep in a way.

I had a significant amount of transference with Dorothy. Through psychodynamic counseling she helped me understand the benefits and drawbacks of wishing for something in a place where I could not get it. Part of what helped me open up to Dorothy was her ability to convey empathy. When I saw tears welling up in her eyes very early in our relationship, a part of me thought I had finally found the mother I had always wished for. I fantasized about her taking me home and giving my younger self the love I wanted from my parents. Through years of tears, arguments, and tension, Dorothy and I worked through these feelings. One thing that happened over and over was every time I told Dorothy about a new memory from my childhood, I would feel enraged with her. I wanted her to grab a hold of me and hug me and tell me it was going to be okay. I wanted her to love me more because of what happened to me. These sessions were dreadful and painful because I could not accept that she was not able to give me what I wanted. With a lot of determination, we both hung in there, until I was ready to understand why I placed these expectations onto Dorothy. Part of my healing was being able to love the younger part of myself that never got what I needed after I was abused.

In the psychodynamic approach, we learn more about where our feelings are coming from. We learn how to give ourselves some of what we did not get from adults when we were growing up. We learn by speaking about our feelings and being able to name where these feelings are coming from. We learn how to keep feelings of longing and yearning in the past and find people who can love us in the way we need now, as adults.

Instead of putting these wishes onto mother figures, I needed to learn how to mother the part of myself that was hurt. I needed to learn how to tend to my mind, body, and heart when new memories of my abuse surfaced.

We had hundreds of conversations about times when I felt abandoned by my family. We talked at length about the disappointments that would come from taking these wishes and placing them in my relationships as an adult. The psychodynamic therapeutic approach worked best for me because it allowed me to develop an awareness I had never had when I was growing up.

There are a variety of approaches survivors can utilize in their healing journey. What works best for one person may not work at all for another. The key is to have all the information about the different options and then to find a therapist or facility that is equipped to offer the best service, no matter what the strategy.

EMDR (Eye Movement Desensitization and Reprocessing)

What is EMDR? According to the EMDR Institute, it is a "psychotherapy that enables people to heal from the symptoms and emotional distress that are the result of disturbing childhood experiences." The institute goes on to explain that "repeated studies show that by using EMDR therapy people can experience the benefits of psychotherapy that once took years to make a difference."[1] According to several studies, millions of people have been successfully treated using EMDR.

Why do trauma survivors turn to EMDR as a therapeutic intervention? I have met several survivors who have been in therapy for years and report feeling stuck in their healing process. Some clients have told me that talking about what happened to them has not been enough. The goal of EMDR is to lessen the volume of distress, and it also helps make space so the brain can process information without being so overwhelmed. Through EMDR, people can work through trauma until it no longer disrupts or overwhelms them in their lives in the present.

Repeated studies show that adding EMDR therapy can help people experience the benefits of therapy that initially took years to make a difference. The American Psychiatric Association, the World Health Organization, and the Department of Defense now recognize EMDR as an effective form of treatment for trauma.

Francine Shapiro, the originator and developer of EMDR, created an eight-phase treatment. Eye movements are used during the first part of the session. After the therapist determines which memory to focus on first, they ask the client to hold different aspects of that event or thought in mind and to use their eyes to track the therapist's hand as it moves back and forth. When EMDR is done correctly and is successful, the interpretation of the painful childhood event is reframed on an emotional level. For example, a childhood abuse survivor shifts from feeling shame and disgust with the belief that "I survived it and I am strong." Many survivors who have utilized this technique have told me that they have been transformed and that they think differently than in the past. Francine Shapiro talked extensively in her book about how EMDR leaves clients feeling empowered versus feeling defeated and worthless.[2] Shapiro and other trauma experts do not recommend using this technique if a client is actively engaged in drug or alcohol misuse. It is difficult to use EMDR if the person has not learned how to create safety in their current relationships.

I worked with one client—I will call her Samantha—who started seeing me when she was eighteen years old, months after being date raped. She developed a raging eating disorder, in addition to PTSD and other self-destructive behaviors. She was unable to form healthy connections with peers. Samantha was abandoned on a street corner days after her mother gave birth to her. She spent her first six months of life in another country, stranded in an adoption center.

From the age of eighteen through her early twenties, Samantha went from one inpatient psychiatric facility to the next. All her therapists reported that she lacked a sense of self and that she really struggled to connect with others. Her emotions were muted. Many of her group members at a variety of facilities reported that she was "vacant." Samantha was always such a likable young woman, but she was unable to talk about anything other than superficial topics. She connected with several males who took advantage of her after the date rape. While Samantha knew she wanted a meaningful relationship with a guy, she had no idea what was getting in her way or why she lacked a sense of worth. For months Samantha worked with an adoption specialist in addition to me and other outpatient therapists. She began to make connections between her abandonment by her biological mother and her inability to formulate attachments in the present. After spending a couple of years in and out of inpatient psychiatric facilities, Samantha and her family decided to pursue treatment in a longer-term residential setting that offered several different therapeutic modalities.

Once she settled into her latest long-term program, her therapist suggested that she use EMDR to gain insight into her attachment issues and lack of self-worth. When Samantha was discharged back to outpatient, she and I discussed the value of using EMDR. Samantha told me that reprocessing experiences when she pushed away family and friends helped her feel less shame and guilt about the emotional pain she caused her family.

Samantha reported that she noticed a significant difference in her mood and overall outlook after completing a dozen EMDR sessions. When she had memories of inflicting self-harm or lashing out at her parents, she no longer reported feeling like a "horrible daughter." She told me that she can look back at this time in her life and make sense of the choices she was making at the time. Samantha realized that she was using self-destructive coping mechanisms because she believed at some point everyone would abandon her. She gained insight into the purpose of these behaviors, and instead of shaming herself, she moved into self-compassion. She was able to forgive herself for choices that caused others harm.

What Is DBT?

Dialectical Behavior Therapy (DBT) is a type of psychotherapy that is based on cognitive behavioral therapy (CBT). Unlike CBT, DBT specifically focuses on helping people who experience emotions very deeply. CBT helps people understand how their thoughts affect their emotions. Dialectical means combining opposite ideas. This strategy was developed in the 1970s by Dr. Marsha Linehan. Initially Dr. Linehan developed this therapy approach to help women who were suicidal. According to the National Library of Medicine, "Linehan weaved into the treatment interventions designed to convey acceptance of the patient and to help the patient accept herself, her emotions, thoughts, the world, and others. As such, DBT came to rest on a foundation of dialectical philosophy, whereby therapists strive to continually balance and synthesize acceptance and change-oriented strategies."[3]

Throughout my years working as a clinician, I have had multiple clients who have attended a variety of intensive outpatient and day programs utilizing the DBT approach. Childhood abuse survivors struggle with accepting their history and all the crazy-making emotions that come with integrating their earlier traumas. Often survivors struggle with immense feelings of shame and rage. When clients report chronic feelings of suicidality, self-harming behaviors, substance use disorders, eating disorders, or crippling anxiety or depression, I have recommended DBT.

The main goal of DBT is to find a balance between acceptance of who you are and the challenges you face as you make changes in the present. The structure of DBT varies among therapists, but generally it involves four types of sessions. The process begins with a preassessment, followed by individual therapy sessions, a skills-training therapy group, and telephone crisis management in between sessions.

Individual therapy sessions have four goals. The first goal is to keep you safe by helping reduce suicidal or self-harming behaviors. The second goal is to limit behaviors that get in the way of therapy being productive. For example, if rage and shame take over the session, DBT helps to shift and contain those emotions. The third goal is to help clients with self-sabotaging tendencies. For example, DBT helps clients that are repeating patterns of attracting people who are demeaning, narcissistic, or emotionally unavailable. The last goal of DBT therapy is to help clients replace unhealthy behaviors with mindfulness and self-care strategies.

DBT therapists often recommend that clients keep a journal to track their emotions and actions and to look for repeated patterns of self-destructive behaviors. DBT skills training in groups helps to improve daily living by utilizing four skills: mindfulness, distress tolerance, interpersonal effectiveness, and emotion regulation.

One of the most helpful DBT techniques helps clients reframe how they think. For example, instead of saying, "I am a misfit and I do not fit in," clients say, "What happened to me is not normal and I belong just like everyone else!" Another example is when clients say, "I am a failure, or I am worthless." In DBT this is rephrased as "Sometimes I succeed, and when I do well, I will do better the next time."

The four main skills with DBT are distress tolerance, mindfulness, emotion regulation, and interpersonal effectiveness. When people get overwhelmed with PTSD symptoms, they may turn to substance abuse or other self-destruction actions to give themselves instant relief. Turning to destructive mechanisms in the moment may provide relief, but in the long run these methods end up causing more emotional pain. Some of the coping strategies used to manage distress tolerance are distracting from negative thoughts, accepting what you cannot change and focus on what you can change, self-soothing practices, imagining yourselves in a safe, peaceful place, and turning to spirituality.

Mindfulness is also incorporated into DBT methodology. These skills include being more in the moment, observing your thoughts and feelings without judgment, breathing exercises, and being kind and compassionate. Emotion regulation skills are especially helpful when there is a childhood history that involves feeling threatened or abandoned. Managing emotional dysregulation includes recognizing your emotions, understanding how your thoughts and behaviors influence your emotions, gaining awareness about self-destructive behaviors, and increasing positive feelings. The last skills included in DBT are about improving interpersonal effectiveness skills. This includes gaining insight into how others feel, using assertiveness instead of passive-aggressive behaviors, being more direct about what you need, and using active listening when engaging with others.

There are many benefits of using DBT as part of the healing journey. I have observed dozens of clients who have seen a reduction of self-harming behaviors, less substance abuse, and improved mood. I worked with one client, whom I will call Amy, who attended an intensive outpatient program that used DBT. Amy was in therapy on and off for most of her twenties. We worked together for eight years doing weekly therapy sessions. Amy's childhood was inundated with abandonment, abuse, and neglect. Her mother was narcissistic, and her father was physically and emotionally abusive. Amy struggled with feelings of worthlessness, and she had suicidal tendencies for years. When I met Amy around the age of twenty-eight, she was dating an older man who treated her poorly. He often belittled her, and he took advantage of her. Amy revealed years into our therapy that this man was stealing her money and crashing in her apartment after he lost one job after another.

Amy yearned to be with a man that would give her attention. She thought that if she gave him whatever he wanted, that he would give back love and validation. Amy had a pattern of being attracted to men who were emotionally unavailable or verbally abusive. When Amy turned thirty years old, she decided she needed to give her childhood abuse history more attention. Amy spent about one year incorporating DBT treatment into her healing journey. She developed skills to manage her suicidal thoughts. She learned how to reframe her self-deprecating feelings. As the months went by, I noticed a big shift in Amy. She was starting to set boundaries and say no. She broke off the relationship with the man that basically just took all of what he wanted. Amy wanted to be in a healthy relationship with a man and eventually wanted a family of her own. Her dedication to herself and her worth allowed her to take risks at work and in her personal life. She got a job promotion, and she started dating a man that cared about her. Amy told me that DBT "saved [her] life." She went on to explain that the combination of reframing and mindfulness skills helped her to stay present, and to be able to manage triggers when she felt abandoned. Amy and several other of my clients who have used DBT have told me that for the first time ever, their life was worth living.

What Is Internal Family Systems (IFS)

Internal family systems is another approach to therapy that helps survivors identify different subpersonalities or families within each person's mental system. These subpersonalities consist of wounded parts and painful feelings such as shame or anger. These parts try to control and protect the person from feeling the anguish associated with these parts. IFS was developed by psychologist Richard Schwartz. In his work as a therapist, Schwartz observed patterns and how people described their "inner lives, the conflicted subpersonalities that resided within them."[4]

Schwartz described the mind as a family, and he developed IFS to help survivors understand how these family members interacted with each other.

IFS is a form of talk therapy, and the therapist helps the client identify the three common roles and how they interact with each other. The three common roles are the managers, which are the parts that try and control people's surroundings and manage emotions so people can function in their daily lives. The exiles are the parts that hold the fear and shame from the abuse. The manager's role is to try and keep the exiles buried and out of consciousness. The firefighters get activated when the exiles feel overwhelmed or threatened. Firefights try and inhibit these difficult emotions, which often results in substance use or binge eating.

Dr. Schwartz reiterated that everyone has a core self, or a part of them, that is wanted to be accessed. The self is what helps people identify, observe, and help these parts become less destructive and more productive. The goal of IFS is to help people get in touch with their core self and free themselves from the parts that lead to disconnection and destructive coping mechanisms. In other words, IFS strives to help people coordinate their parts, so they work together and allow the self to be in charge.

There are a variety of treatment modalities survivors can implement into their healing journey. There is no right or wrong way to approach treatment. The most important factor is safety and knowing where you are in the process of recovering. I would not recommend EMDR to someone who has not addressed their childhood trauma. I would recommend EMDR to someone who has done extensive therapy around their abuse history and feels stuck in the impact of their experience. I would not recommend DBT to someone who benefits from speaking and telling their story in a safe setting. DBT does not focus on talking about the past. This strategy helps people stay grounded and in the present. I have worked with many survivors who buried years of memories and feelings. For them, psychodynamic therapy is an effective way to explore the source of their symptoms and challenging situations. This therapy investigates the "why" behind our thoughts and actions. Questions such as "Why am I feeling this way?" or "Where is that feeling coming from?" help us understand the root of the emotion and where to place it.

ALTERNATIVE FORMS OF COPING

Somatic Experiencing

Throughout the years clinicians and survivors have developed a host of alternative forms of coping when therapy is not enough. Somatic experiencing, referred to as SE, is a body-oriented therapeutic strategy that can be applied in multiple professional settings. Many people with abuse histories experience living disconnected from their bodies. SE is a body-oriented therapy that helps people identify where in their bodies they go into fight, flight, or freeze mode. Dr. Peter Levine, who founded SE, says, "The Somatic Experiencing method works to release this stored energy and turn off this threat alarm that causes severe dysregulation and dissociation. SE helps people understand this body response to trauma and work through a 'body first' approach to healing."[5]

Trauma-Informed Yoga

Trauma-informed yoga is geared toward students who have had some kind of trauma in their lives. Yoga is supposed to heal, but for survivors it can cause emotional harm or distress when the space for healing is also triggering. For example, some yoga teachers offer hands-on assistance as students are doing different poses. Trauma-informed yoga teachers are trained to be aware of trauma and understand how PTSD can affect someone's practice. For example, an instructor who has been trauma-informed trained will not touch a student during the class without getting permission. One instructor that I work with has a card that she places next to each student. Throughout the classes, attendees can decide if they want to be touched by the instructor, indicating that by the position of the card. One side is red, and the other side of the card is green. This empowers students to give themselves the option of having physical contact with the instructor. This type of yoga increases body awareness in a safe setting, and it can facilitate feelings of physical, emotional, and psychological safety.

Physical Activities

Physical activities, such as rock climbing, hiking or mountain biking may work better for some people. I spoke to one client, whom I will call Mary, who described mountain biking as a form of moving meditation. Mary struggled with bouts of major depressive episodes with dissociative tendencies for decades. When she was in her mid-forties she began biking after meeting another woman who was also a childhood abuse survivor. On many occasions Mary did her therapy sessions in the parking lot of her next adventure. She spent hours at a time on the trails following our sessions. Mary told me that having to focus on specific details and tasks ahead are "what keep me in my body." She went on to say, "It is my safe place." I saw a significant change in Mary as she added biking to her healing journey. She was more confident and more present. Mary began using her voice more with her colleagues and her girlfriend. Her mood was brighter, and she reported less dissociative episodes. She was ecstatic when I told her I wanted to share her example in this book. Mary struggled for years to find peace in her body.

Journaling

When we find alternative coping strategies that work for us, we often rely on them to help us cope with feelings of anger, fear, shame, and despair. Over half of the clients I have worked with have used journaling as another alternative coping strategy. Expressive writing helps moderate symptoms of PTSD. Keeping a thoughtful diary or a journal can be a vital tool for adults who are remembering or revisiting memories of childhood abuse. For about ten years I carried around a notebook, and every time I had a new memory, or I was triggered, I wrote down what I remembered and what I felt.

I brought that notebook to hundreds of sessions. I shared some journal entries with Dorothy. There were times when I literally could not speak. I was full of shame and fear about what I remembered. When I fell silent in sessions, I would hand Dorothy my notebook. I watched her read whatever I shared with her. I took notice of her teary eyes and look of concern as she read my words. Dorothy always asked me, "How did it feel to share that?" She showed interest in what I had to say and never made me feel like I was crazy after I shared a new memory or revelation. I believe that writing in my notebook kept me out of the hospital. When I was considering suicide or inundated with shame, I would write down the reasons why I should not act on those feelings. I also wrote down different thoughts I could say to myself when I wanted to quit. For example, I wrote down things like, "I can do this," "I have so much to live for," or "I love Dorothy."

Effective journaling is a way to tell ourselves what we are thinking and feeling, without having to worry about other people's judgments. When we go back and reread what we wrote, we gain insight and understanding into our feelings, which can improve our mood and our outlook on our journey moving forward. We are more likely to tell the truth when we write it down. On several occasions I wrote down, "I was raped," "I am not making this up," and "My body remembers everything that was done to me, and no one can take that away."

Finding a Trauma-Informed Therapist

As we explore all the different therapeutic modalities and alternative forms of coping, we need to consider how to find the right therapist. All these forms of treatment are most beneficial when we are working with a trauma-informed therapist. The five principles associated with trauma-informed therapy are safety, choice, collaboration, trustworthiness, and empowerment. Trauma-informed therapists are extremely sensitive to helping their clients manage traumatic reactions. Several of my colleagues who work with trauma warriors tell me that "we are the hardest working set of individuals they have ever met." Childhood abuse survivors are seen by trauma-informed therapists as unique individuals who have experienced extremely abnormal events. Dorothy always told me, "It is not you that is not normal. It is what happened to you, that is not normal." Statements like this reduce shame and help clients feel hopeful that their lives can be "normal," even after surviving crazy-making experiences as children.

If you think that trauma-informed care is a good fit for you, seek therapy from someone with the appropriate training. Request a brief phone call with two or three qualified therapists. If you know other people who are in therapy for PTSD, ask those people for recommendations. Write down a list of questions. Here are some things you can ask to determine if the therapist is a potential match.

1. What training have you done?

2. Do you consider yourself trauma-informed?

3. What is your approach to therapy when working with clients who have a trauma history?

4. What kinds of clients do you work with or what kinds of trauma have you helped people heal from?

5. Do you feel comfortable working with clients who have a history of childhood abuse? Do you feel comfortable working with clients who have suicidal tendencies, self-harming behaviors, or substance use disorders?

6. How often do you see your clients per week? Are you available to check in via phone or email when clients are in crisis?

CHAPTER 4

The Role of Self-Destructive
Tendencies after Childhood Abuse

WHAT THE RESEARCH IS SAYING ABOUT THE ROLE OF SELF-DESTRUCTIVE BEHAVIORS

Research indicates that all types of childhood abuse are associated with an increased risk to develop self-destructive behaviors, such as eating disorders and substance abuse disorders.[1] We start forming an opinion of our reality very early in life. Our view of the world is largely based on our connection with our parents, siblings, other family members, caretakers, teachers, and other adults in a position of authority. When we were growing up, we depended on our caregivers for survival. It is virtually impossible for most of us to accept that our caregiver or loved adult was abusing us or was a bad person.

When children do complain or report possible maltreatment, they are often told things like, "They are your parents, they would not do that" or "How dare you talk badly about your mother or father." We continue to live in a culture that protects parents and caregivers. While there is more education and resources for children living in unsafe environments, society would rather disbelieve children because most people do not want to think that a caregiver or parent has the capacity to hurt children intentionally or is ill equipped to provide love in an appropriate way.

Decades before childhood abuse was widely discussed, a study led by Bessel van der Kolk and Judith Herman suggested that many adults who act out self-destructive behaviors have also had a history of abuse and disrupted parental care.[2] Subjects diagnosed with personality disorders or bipolar II disorder were monitored over four years for suicide attempts, self-injury, and eating disorders. These behaviors were connected to self-reported histories of childhood abuse by all the subjects in the study. Van der Kolk and Herman found significant predictors of cutting and suicide attempts were linked to histories of neglect and abuse during childhood. Their findings validated and continue to support that childhood abuse survivors are at higher risk of self-harm when they reexperience or interpret events in the present as rejection, abusive, or neglectful.[3]

When I talk to clients about how they interpreted abusive behaviors done to them by adults, they often tell me things like "I had no idea I was being mistreated." On numerous occasions I have witnessed my clients realizing through therapy that what happened to them as children was abusive or neglectful treatment.

For example, I worked with one female client in her thirties—I will call her Marni—who came to therapy because of multiple suicide attempts and self-harm. Early in our relationship, Marni shared with me that she had constantly considered suicide after she moved away to college. Marni witnessed her siblings being beaten by her mother. She also told me that her mother threw her down the steps after she broke a window with her soccer ball. When I asked Marni if she thought this was an appropriate way to discipline, she told me, "I did not know any different. I thought all kids got beat by their parents when they did something wrong."

When Marni started therapy, she had not made the connection between her past and her extensive history of self-harm and self-loathing. Marni told me she did not understand why she was depressed, and she did not have insight into her self-injurious behaviors. When we started working together Marni told me she had never had a relationship with an adult that was "nice." During her early adulthood she was attracted to a string of abusive men and women in her personal and professional life. About a year after Marni started therapy, she began reading the book *The Body Keeps the Score*.[4] As Marni read the book, she processed in therapy the insights and connections she was able to make between her traumatic childhood and her tendency to cause harm to herself when she was triggered.

Like most survivors, Marni internalized the behaviors of her mother. She assumed that she was the one in the wrong and that all children get beat when they misbehave. As children get older, they develop unconscious or conscious beliefs that they are unlovable.

Most childhood abuse survivors have had thoughts like "Why don't people love me?" or "Why didn't my parents protect me?" Many of us have also asked ourselves, "Why did my abuser hurt me like that?" Research indicates that these thoughts left unaddressed lead to feelings of rage, despair, betrayal, and fear. As time goes on, the pain and rejection piles up inside of our hearts, minds, and bodies. In order to understand self-destructive tendencies or suicidal thoughts in adulthood, we need to rewire that part of our brain that convinced us that the world is bad and that we cannot trust other people. Living in a constant state of hypervigilance leads to a life of isolation and emptiness.

During the last five years there has been extensive research on men and women reporting a history of all types of childhood abuse and then going on to struggling with eating disorders or dependency on drugs or alcohol. According to the New York Center for Eating Disorders, 50 percent of all patients diagnosed with an eating disorder have a history of childhood abuse. Unlike people, food feels safe. Food does not abuse or abandon people. Food is the most available, legal, and socially acceptable mood-lifting drug on the market. Dozens of my clients have reported that they used symptoms of an eating disorder during their childhood.

I started bingeing on sweets when I was around ten years old. I would plan what I would eat as I drifted off in school. I would come home after school and raid my refrigerator, or I would take my bike to the local convenience store and buy candy. During my adolescence, my relationship with food took a turn. Instead of bingeing, I started counting calories, and I obsessed about losing weight. When I was fourteen years old, I lost over ten pounds. My parents told me how great I looked, and my father told me he admired my self-restraint with food. My life felt so out of control from trying to bury memories of sexual abuse and unwanted pregnancies, which at the time I did not know were pregnancies. While my relationship with food was destructive, it served a purpose. I would refer to my eating disorder as my secret keeper and my confidence booster. It was not until I started therapy with Dorothy that I started to understand the role of my eating disorder. I realized that my destructive tendencies helped me to stay sane and feel confident in a body that at the time was being destroyed.

I worked with one woman, now in her fifties, whom I will call Pam. She grew up without a mother. She was sexually abused as a child by her older brother. Pam talked in therapy about how food was the only thing she could control growing up. She talked about memories of when she would stand in front of a table full of sweets and that she would ruminate on what to eat next. Years into therapy she realized that food took the place of her absent mother. For Pam, food became the source of object permanence and love. Food never left her or belittled her. Food comforted her when she longed to have a mother object. Pam and most clients I have treated continue to use destructive eating patterns into their adulthood.

Adults who were sexually abused as children are also at higher risk of developing an addiction to drugs or alcohol. In one study of clients in an inpatient drug treatment center, research showed that 72 percent of those clients reported a form of sexual abuse during childhood.[5] Survivors turn to drugs or alcohol to numb the shame, pain, and fear associated with their trauma history. In most cases, people with addiction disorders do not have insight or understand the connection of abusing drugs to their abuse history.

Adults who have experienced one-time physical abuse or prolonged, on-going physical abuse as children are at higher risk of developing an addiction. The National Institute on Drug Abuse found that two-thirds of people in rehab for drug abuse reported being physically abused as children.[6] Several studies have reported that emotional abuse and neglect are often closely linked to early exposure to drugs or alcohol abuse from the parent or caregiver. Data from the Department of Health and Human Services reported that between 30 and 60 percent of all child abuse cases involved substance use.

Most of my clients who have survived emotional or physical abuse also lived with a parent who was addicted to a substance. Marni, who I mentioned survived physical and emotional abuse, also lived with an addicted parent. Whenever she talked in therapy about her memories, she also told me that her mother "was always drunk." Marni said the next day she would act like nothing happened. Marni believed that her mother had little memory of some of the incidents because she was so intoxicated at the time the abuse occurred. Throughout her childhood, no one explained to Marni the pathology in her family and how that affected her mother's treatment of her. No one helped Marni develop coping strategies during the years she was abused. No one told Marni that she was not the cause of her mother's choices.

CHAPTER 4

UNDERSTANDING THE ROLE OF AN EATING DISORDER AND ADDICTION

Eating disorders often develop from a need to take control of one's environment. This coping mechanism can be triggered by a traumatic experience that occurred in one's childhood. The biggest predictors of eating disorders in adulthood are emotional abuse, physical abuse, sexual abuse, and neglect by parents or adults who did not protect them during childhood.

No one chooses to have an eating disorder or become addicted to drugs or alcohol. When children are being abused, they gravitate toward numbing strategies because they are not equipped to process their feelings or emotions. They step into survival mode, and many resort to dissociative tendencies to disconnect from their experience.

Most of my clients who have childhood abuse histories also exhibit dissociative tendencies early in treatment. I worked with one woman in her thirties—I will refer to her as Debbie—who began therapy after discharging from a residential eating disorders treatment center. When Debbie reached out to me, she told me she had begun battling bulimia and binge eating disorder symptoms at age seventeen. Initially, Debbie reported that the role of her eating disorder was to cope with the death of her father. When I spoke to her inpatient therapist, she told me she believed Debbie had been using symptoms of bulimia because she never processed her feelings about her father's death. Debbie's therapist explained that the role of her eating disorder was to keep people at arm's length, to avoid losing anyone else in her life. She told me that Debbie was so afraid of losing other family members to illness that she gradually disconnected from anyone who knew her father.

When I met Debbie, she was reserved, and her affect was flat. At the time, she told me her therapeutic goals were to stabilize her mood and develop alternative coping strategies to manage her depression. It seemed to me that Debbie was ready to let go of her eating disorder. I met Debbie when she was in her early thirties. At that time, she told me she wanted to start a family. She got married before she entered the inpatient facility. About a year into our therapy, Debbie's mood improved. She had greatly reduced usage of all her bulimic symptoms. She got pregnant with her first child in our second year of working together. Debbie was able to experience her pregnancy without using any symptoms of her eating disorder. Her depression seemed to be a thing of the past.

About three months postpartum, Debbie's mood took a sudden turn for the worse. She began using laxatives after being symptom free throughout her pregnancy. I noticed that her affect in the session was disconnected. She stopped making eye contact, and she started reporting gaps in missing time. Debbie told me, "I am losing hours of my day. I find myself drifting off, especially when I am driving." We began talking about dissociation, and Debbie was able to identify that she had struggled with that coping strategy on and off for years.

I had learned earlier in my career as a therapist that people do not start dissociating in adulthood. In most cases, dissociation is seen in adults who have experienced some type of trauma early in life. A few weeks after I noticed this symptom with Debbie, I reached out to some colleagues and my therapist. When I saw Debbie's eyes become glazed, and when I could feel myself drifting when I sat in session with her, I was aware that she looked a lot like I did when I was seeing Dorothy and still repressing memories of childhood abuse.

Once Debbie and I could acknowledge that dissociation was part of her symptomatology, we were able to better understand the role of her eating disorder. When Debbie realized she was beginning to slip into a relapse, she was determined to not let her eating disorder disrupt this next chapter of her life as a new mother. Gradually, Debbie opened up about her relationship with her mother and father. Debbie reported having flashbacks, nightmares, and psychosomatic complaints as memories of her abuse history became conscious. She was having migraines, chronic itching, and back pain. When I asked her what her body was trying to tell her, she said repeatedly, "Something is really wrong."

Here is one of the first questions I ask clients when they talk about their gut feelings: "Is this a familiar feeling?" When I asked Debbie that question, she described having awful dread when she woke up some mornings as a child. When Debbie spoke about the pain and disorientation she felt as she woke up, I could remember times when I felt the same way. It occurred to me that Debbie may have been doing the same thing I did growing up. As I progressed in my trauma therapy, I recognized that the morning after my father sexually abused me, my brain unconsciously pushed away the memory, but my body was storing the emotions until I was ready to confront my past in adulthood. For years I resorted to anorexic and obsessive food tendencies to bury the truth. Years into my treatment I learned that part of the role of my eating disorder was to make my abuse not so. I would have done anything to keep up the facade that I had a great family and a "normal" childhood. I obsessed about my food intake and tried to shrink my physical body to make all the flashbacks and body memories disappear.

As Debbie and I progressed into this part of her healing process, I thought about the role of my eating disorder, and I also reflected on the work I had done with dozens of other clients who had figured out the role of their eating disorder. While I knew Debbie was stepping into extremely painful territory, I also felt like she needed to let herself know the truth so she could say goodbye to her eating disorder.

Throughout the next several months of our therapy, Debbie cautiously began speaking about the "real" relationship she had with her father before he passed away. Debbie told me that she loved her father, but that he also "really creeped me out." She described many times as a child when she would go out of her way to avoid him. She told me if she heard him walking down the hallway, she would hide in her closet. She uncovered that she felt suicidal when she was approaching her teens. Debbie also remembered that her eating disorder started when she began developing a woman's body. At the time Debbie did not know that she was trying to get rid of the parts of her body that were being violated by her father.

It took Debbie several years in therapy to come to terms with her relationship with her father and mother. As Debbie allowed herself to find words for her childhood trauma history, her eating disorder symptoms dissipated. When Debbie wanted to forget what she had already remembered, she would use her bulimia. There were times in our work that Debbie shut down and resorted back to her eating disorder. Each time Debbie climbed her way out of despair she learned more about why she had held onto her eating disorder until her forties. Debbie continues to explore her childhood and how she shoved years of pain and shame into her body. However, she has gained much insight into her coping strategies, and she has learned how to identify what her eating disorder urges are bringing to her attention. When she wants to gravitate toward bulimia, she asks herself, "What purpose does this serve in my life now?"

Actionable Steps You Can Take to Understand the Role of Your Eating Disorder

1. Grab your journal and start writing about the role of your eating disorder. Some journal prompts to consider are:

    a. Do you remember when the eating disorder came to life? How would you describe your eating disorder? For example, is it your best friend, enemy, or both? How does your eating disorder protect you from feelings about your abuse? What kind of relationship do you want to have with food and your body?

b. Write a letter to your eating disorder. Talk about the role it has served throughout the years and if you want to continue to hold onto it. Does it serve as your voice? Does it make you feel safe? Does it help you avoid your feelings? Is it working?

c. What steps can you take to let go of your eating disorder? Do you need more help from a professional? What are the benefits of understanding the role of your eating disorder? Will it bring you more joy or peace? What feelings or beliefs about your abuse hold you back from saying goodbye to your eating disorder?

2. Join a support group with other men and women who have similar histories. Preferably a group that is composed of survivors of childhood abuse and facilitated by a trauma therapist.

3. Do the opposite of what you are used to doing when you have memories, flashbacks, and/or nightmares. If it is normal for you to resort to eating disorder behaviors when PTSD is surging, try something different. Remind yourself of your choices. For example, if you are having urges to use a symptom of your eating disorder, call a friend, go for a hike, write in your journal, reach out to a trusted professional, or watch a funny show.

4. If you have identified that your eating disorder acts as a friend or comfort during times of despair and pain, consider replacing your eating disorder with nurturing relationships. Think about the people you have in your life, and what they can offer. Friends listen. Friends accept us for who we are. Friends do not shame us for our history. Friends hold onto hope when we feel like we want to give up. Friends want us to be healthy and happy. Food cannot offer us love or attention in the way that we need it. Understand that it takes time

to find quality, trustworthy relationships. It is a process. It is okay to give yourself time to find ways to replace your eating disorder with people that care about you.

Survivors of childhood abuse may also turn to different types of addictive substances or behaviors. Addictions can come in the form of a sex addiction, excessive gambling, workaholism, over-exercising, food, drugs, and/or alcohol. The correlation between child abuse and substance use disorder is strong, but the direct cause is not always clear. Children who grow up in abusive or neglectful environments may dabble with substance use or alcohol use in their prepubescent years. The pain and stress that comes from childhood abuse can lead to an addiction. There are long-term emotional and psychological problems that affect survivors years into their adulthood, especially if they have not received mental health support during or after these types of traumas have occurred. Common emotions linked to addictive tendencies include repressed anger, feeling trapped, lack of self-worth, and a need to escape.

I have worked with hundreds of clients who struggle with emotion regulation and impulse control problems. Emotion regulation is the process people use to moderate all types of feelings and behaviors in response to triggers. A lack of emotion regulation in adulthood may be a result of witnessing parents or caretakers in childhood with the inability to contain feelings or respond appropriately in times of stress. For example, children who are physically or emotionally abused by adults learn from a young age that anger is expressed through violence or degradation. It is not uncommon for a substance to be utilized by an adult who inflicts harm on their child.

I have worked with many clients who come to therapy because they want to stay sober and let go of their substance use disorder. Many of these clients have reported an inability to manage their anger at work and in their personal relationships. When my clients have started therapy, they often lack awareness between their emotion dysregulation and how that has put them at much higher risk of becoming addicted to a substance.

In order to let go of any destructive coping mechanism, we need to understand where it comes from. When I begin counseling survivors with a substance use disorder, I often start by asking them to write out a timeline of critical events in their childhoods. On this timeline, clients list traumatic childhood events, how they coped with what happened, and how other family members reacted. For example, one of my clients—I will call her Cathy—started therapy in her early twenties after surviving emotional and physical abuse by her mother and physical abuse by her father. When I met Cathy, she barely spoke about her childhood. She focused mostly on her perfectionistic tendencies. She was in a master's program for counseling. Cathy still lived at home when she began treatment with me.

After about six months of weekly counseling, Cathy gradually began sharing more about her family life growing up. She spoke about her relationship with her mother. Cathy described her mother as "judgy and critical." One day she entered my office hysterically crying. Cathy told me she had gotten a B- on an exam. Cathy told me her mother reacted as if she had done something terribly wrong. She was sobbing, telling me she felt like a failure. I explored with her where that feeling came from. I asked her, "When did you learn that being less than perfect was a bad thing?" With surprise on her face, she told me that her parents were extremely critical of her performance in school. I asked her to write out a timeline of when she felt like she had let people down.

Cathy came back to session the next week with a poster board full of times when she felt like a failure. She listed dates going back to her elementary school years. When Cathy was in sixth grade, she was grounded for a week for getting a C on a math test. On the timeline she wrote, "My mom told me I was stupid and that I would never amount to anything." Cathy went on to write that her father "went on a rant and that he threw her across the room when he came home from work that night." Cathy included more recent events when she was in college as well. She wrote about one night when she had received a B on a research paper in one of her psychology classes. Her comments about how her parents reacted were very similar to the event in the sixth grade. As we discussed different events from her high school and college years, Cathy noticed a trend and the development of her addiction to alcohol. She told me that when she felt beaten up or shamed by her parents, she would turn to wine to numb her feelings.

On her timeline, Cathy also included what she felt in her body when these abusive episodes occurred. Cathy described feeling like her head was going to explode. She wrote on the timeline, "I feel like my blood is boiling and I just wanted to make it stop." Cathy also wrote about feeling like her heart was breaking. When I asked her more about that she told me that she could not wrap her head around how a parent could "treat me like this."

As Cathy got older, she knew that what was going on in her home was not typical. She spent a lot of time at a friend's house in high school. Cathy talked about her relationship with some of the other mothers in her friend group. When Cathy told her friends about her mother's tyrants of belittling and her father's raging tendencies, her friends offered a bed for her at their homes.

When Cathy and I were working through her childhood traumas and trying to address her self-destructive tendencies with alcohol, one of her grandparents fell ill. Cathy talked a lot in therapy about her "grandpa." She told me he was her cheerleader, and that nothing she did was less than perfect in his eyes, even if she received an average grade or did not perform at her best in sports.

During our second year in therapy Cathy's grandpa passed away. She was heartbroken. Her depression and PTSD symptoms became more severe. She had more episodes of despondency, and she had several more flashbacks from her early childhood.

Unfortunately, her grandfather's death led her down a more destructive path with alcohol and drugs. She began using opioids to push away the unbearable emotional pain. Initially, Cathy hesitated to talk openly in therapy about her drug abuse dependency.

She started missing therapy sessions and avoided in-person contact with many of her friends. Cathy spent most of her time hiding in her bedroom in her parents' home. I noticed that she was less forthcoming in our sessions, and she often looked away when she talked to me. I asked her to write a letter to her grandfather, trying to express what his death meant to her.

Over the course of months Cathy shared more about her history of abuse and how she turned to drugs and alcohol when memories of her abuse were activated. She began to piece together that she tried to numb the fight-or-flight response when she was attempting to connect with others, especially potential intimate partners. Cathy also made the connection between the loss of her grandfather and how she resorted to substances to replace the safety she felt when she spent time with her grandfather. Like all of us, Cathy yearned to feel loved and accepted. When her life at home felt chaotic or unsafe, Cathy held onto her connection with her grandfather. On several occasions Cathy told me, "If it weren't for my grandpa and the love he showed me, I do not think I would still be here."

One of the biggest indicators to addictive behaviors is the wish to rid ourselves of any pain or uncomfortable emotion the second we begin to feel it. The rush of endorphins that comes from substances or other addictive behaviors is a vicious cycle that requires on-going attention. Having a history of childhood abuse affects our attachment. It affects how we perceive those we are in relationships with and impacts our relationship with ourselves. Gabor Maté, who is a leading expert in the addiction field says that "an addiction manifests in any behavior that a person finds temporary pleasure or relief in and therefore craves, suffers negative consequences from, and has trouble giving up."[7]

Actionable Steps to Become Sober and Heal from Childhood Abuse

1. Therapy is one of the most effective and safest ways to do this. With the guidance of a therapist, it is possible to link our current behaviors and feelings with what happened to us in the past.

2. Knowing what happened to you is one thing. But when you deeply understand how it shapes who you are, you are beginning to unpick the mystery. Discovering how your brain associated with situations and stimuli based on your experiences is the first (and biggest) step to reducing the effects of childhood trauma.

3. Find a new passion. Take all that time and energy you put into your destructive behaviors and replace that with activities that give you a feeling of freedom, peace, and self-worth. The goal is to replace unhealthy behaviors with healthier ones!

4. Address your addiction. Consider using a twelve-step program in conjunction with your therapy. Look for groups that are tailored toward adults who have survived childhood abuse.

5. Focus on stabilizing your symptoms before diving into any type of trauma work. You need to be sober to effectively work through your childhood issues.

6. Find a professional that understands the connection between addiction and childhood abuse.

7. Work with your therapist or a professional to rid your life of toxic people, toxic emotions, and destructive behaviors. As you distance yourself from people that are or have caused you harm, you will not live life in a constant state of fight or flight.

8. Consider using all or any of these types of therapies to get sober and dig deeper into your past. EMDR, equine-assisted therapy, nutritional counseling, group therapy, and neurofeedback are all strategies that you can utilize on your healing journey.

CHAPTER 5

Grieving Your Lost Childhood

GRIEVING ALL THAT WAS LOST

How does someone begin to grieve all that was lost in their childhood? Part of the healing process for survivors of childhood abuse is to find a way to acknowledge the past, understand it, and then accept what happened to them. The pain associated with knowing the truth is overwhelming and, in most cases, survivors are unable to face these feelings until years into their adulthood. Finding meaningful connections in the present requires us to grieve the loss of a healthy childhood and recognize that our innocence was taken from us.

You may have lost years of childhood by growing up too fast. You may have lost a sense of security due to neglect and substance use disorders by your caretakers. Allowing yourself to acknowledge this is important. You may not have been able to grieve for these losses during childhood because you were using all your internal coping devices to survive. I have not met a client who has not suffered for years or decades, trying to cope with unresolved and complicated grief from their childhoods.

Once we allow ourselves to know the enormity of what happened to us, and we can name it, we need to find ways to move through the grieving process. We need to figure out how to say goodbye to the idea of childhood and innocence. We need to understand the impact of our earlier life traumas. When most people think of the word grief, they associate that with the loss of a loved one, but grief can be about the loss of something we never had.

What kinds of losses do we need to grieve after childhood abuse?

- My self-esteem suffered.
- My ability to make friends and connect with others suffered.
- My ability to trust myself has been skewed.
- My ability to set boundaries was taken.
- My right to feel safe with family and friends was taken.
- My body was violated.
- My innocence was taken.
- The people who were supposed to protect me growing up betrayed me.
- I lost years of my life in adulthood fighting the truth.
- My health has been compromised by my inability to cope with my past.
- I lost the ability to stay in my body and feel safe in intimate relationships.
- I doubted my ability to be successful.

Grieving is a process. It looks different for everyone. There are phases of grieving that can be attributed to healing from childhood abuse. Being aware of the grief stages can increase compassion and self-understanding. Understanding each of the phases of grieving a stolen childhood can help you better understand your needs and help you prioritize in getting them met.

In the denial phase, we may shut down, avoid, or feel numb when we are trying to connect with others. We may find ourselves distracted and keeping busy to stay out of touch with the truth. When we move into the second phase, anger, we may find ourselves lashing out and feeling irritable and impatient. We may pick fights or turn to drugs or alcohol to mute the buried rage we are storing in our minds and bodies. In the bargaining phase, we may go in and out of awareness or staying connected to the truth. If you notice you are thinking things like "Maybe I made this up" or "Maybe I caused my dad or uncle to hit me." These thoughts confuse us and make us doubt whatever memories or flashbacks we may have already processed. During this phase we may feel an excessive amount of guilt or shame. Depression usually hits us in the fourth stage. We may slip into feelings of hopelessness, despair, and feel a lack of interest in living. Many of my clients report more suicidal tendencies as they move into this stage. Once I spent a couple of years remembering and speaking about my childhood, I experienced more bouts of depression. I wanted to disappear. I wanted to make my abuse not so.

It can take years for us to move into the final stage, acceptance. Like all grief, we can also move in and out of the five stages of grief, depending on what is going on in our lives now. I have worked with clients who have regressed back into denial or bargaining when their abuser is sick or passes away.

On April 12, 2003, my father lost his three-year battle with cancer. He was diagnosed with stage 3 stomach cancer two months after I started remembering the incest. For three years, my father was in and out of surgery and multiple chemotherapy interventions. As his cancer progressed, I continued to remember more about what happened to me. I limited my contact with both of my parents, and I struggled with dissociative features. I had body memories, sometimes all day. I considered suicide often. I lashed out at Dorothy at times. I pushed some of my friends away. I blamed myself for his cancer. I told Dorothy that "[i]f I had kept my mouth shut maybe he would not be sick." I assumed that me remembering what he did to me ultimately led to his death.

Both of my parents tried to make me feel responsible for his illness. They would send me detailed reports of his spreading cancer. They would say things like, "How could you do this to us?" People in my extended family shamed me for speaking and questioned my memories. Many of my family tried to convince me that Dorothy was putting these memories in my head. Throughout these three years of my father's illness, I was unable to move into the final phase of grieving. I realized years later that I was holding onto the hope and wish that he or my mother would take responsibility and acknowledge the past. Once my father passed away, I had to find ways to grieve the kind of relationship that I wanted and never had with my father. I had to accept that he was not willing or able to acknowledge what he did to me, even in his last moments of life.

I was working with another client in her late thirties—I will call her Maureen—who experienced abandonment by her father and neglect by her mother. Maureen's father walked out of her family's life when she was thirteen years old. She told me she came home from school one day and "he was gone." He did not leave an address, a phone number, or a letter saying why he left. Maureen spent pivotal years of her adolescence without a male parental object. She told me that her mother and father never got along, and that she witnessed her father belittling and berating her mother on several occasions. Maureen could not understand why her mother allowed her father to treat her in such a way. When we talked in sessions about her relationship with her father, she would tell me, "I never really had a dad." She told me he did not attend sporting events. She said he was not involved in her life and that "he had no idea what was going on with me." Maureen began to experience depressive symptoms around the same time her father disappeared. She told me her self-esteem was low and that she was attracted to boys who mistreated her in high school.

Maureen realized that she was attracted to boys who had similar qualities as her father.

Once Maureen got her nursing degree and became financially independent, she began dating. She met her husband, whom I will call Bill, when she was twenty years old. Maureen started counseling in her early twenties to address her father's absence and her mother's pathology. Maureen's mother placed high expectations on Maureen to fill the void that was missing with her father. Her mother would talk to her about her financial and emotional distress. Maureen told me, "I became the family therapist." She said she would sit with her sobbing mother and constantly mediate arguments with her brother and mother.

After Maureen's father left, Maureen said she had to rely on her peers or herself when she needed help. She developed bulimia in her mid-teens. After being in therapy for years, Maureen realized that her eating disorder became the replacement for the emotional absence of both of her parents. She knew she yearned for love and safety and consistency, but she did not have the words to describe the losses in her childhood.

Recently, Maureen had to go for several surgeries due to abnormalities in her gynecological makeup. In one year, Maureen had three surgeries. When Maureen came home from her first surgery, she became depressed and more anxious. At first Maureen could not identify the root of her despair. She thought she was reacting to the anesthesia and the pain that followed days after the surgery. Four months after she had two failed procedures, Maureen had to go back for a third surgery.

Throughout this whole process, she never mentioned her mother. I asked her if she had told her mother about the upcoming surgery. Maureen told me, "I am not calling my mom about any surgery. I can't parent her when I need someone to take care of me." For weeks to follow we talked in therapy about the loss of the mother she never had. Maureen moved through the stages of grief, and she allowed herself to feel angry about all the times she felt stranded and unsupported. When Maureen went in for her final surgery, she was at peace. She was able to sit with her sadness about choosing not to include her mother in this part of her journey. Through a lot of tears and anger, Maureen was able to acknowledge and move through her grief about growing up and feeling parentless. Instead of focusing on what was missing, Maureen formed a group of supporters that helped her recover from her last surgery.

Grief of childhood abuse can feel never-ending. Even if we find ourselves free from the abuse itself, the emotions are part of our lives every day. Grief comes in waves. And we have a lot to mourn. One of the most difficult parts of moving through this part of the healing process is dismantling the shame, and making space in our bodies and hearts to say goodbye to our parents or whoever caused us harm. It is unbearably painful to come to terms with the loss of family members who were put into our lives to protect and love us. Our loyalty to our parents or family members keeps us aligned with them. As children, we convince ourselves that we are the cause of the abuse. We are defined by the tribe of people that are supposed to be our caretakers.

An integral part of healing means distancing ourselves from the perpetrators or abusers and reattaching to people outside of our biological tribe. We need to mourn the family that never was. We need to mourn for the lack of accountability, lack of closure, and all that was taken from us. Our families or loved ones failed us in ways that others may not be able to understand.

Coping by hating ourselves as children takes a tremendous toll on us as adults. To explain why our loved ones were abusing us as children, we needed to believe we were unlovable. In order to survive, we blamed ourselves for all the wrong done and we buried our true feelings so that we could survive. In order to love ourselves and reattach to supportive connections in the present, we need to clear out layers of shame.

Actionable Steps to Grieving What Was Lost in Our Childhood

- Give yourself grace and space. Grief is unbearable in some moments.
- Allow yourself to feel your emotions. Take fifteen minutes each day to scream, cry, or express pent-up grief.
- Schedule something every day that brings you joy.
- Talk to someone who understands grief.
- Seek out therapy or specialized grief support groups.
- Tend to your body. Tend to your feelings.
- Don't set a deadline of when you "should" be done grieving.
- Reach out to friends or supportive family members.
- Ask for what you need.
- Set boundaries with difficult people or family members who caused you harm.

DISMANTLING SHAME

People who are consumed with shame after childhood abuse report feeling chronic emptiness or isolation most of the time. I have counseled hundreds of clients who avoid connecting with others because they are afraid that others will see their shame and look at them like they are damaged goods.

The biggest problem with this emotion is that most of us don't want to talk about it. We avoid shame because it makes us feel vulnerable and exposed. But that's a problem, says Brené Brown, who has been researching shame for over two decades.[1] Brown asserts that ignoring shame spreads fear and encourages us to hold onto negative behaviors and thinking.

In her book *Atlas of the Heart*, Brené Brown outlines the three pillars of shame she developed from her own research:[2]

- We all experience shame. It is universal. It is a primitive emotion shared by everyone unless they completely lack empathy[3] or the capacity for human connection.

- It's not easy to talk about shame. Even mentioning the word "shame" can lead to an experience of the emotion and evoke a strong sense of fear.

- Talking about shame brings a sense of control. That control gives us the strength to overcome our feelings and move forward with our lives.

Once we get caught in the shame spiral, there are things we need to do to break the cycle. You can talk to someone you love, reach out to someone you trust, and you can tell your story. Brown points out that shame cannot survive if it is being spoken and being met with empathy.[4] Brown goes on to explain that secrecy, silence, and judgment allows our shame to grow and that the antidote to shame is empathy.

Think about what triggers shame for you. Is it your appearance, your memories, your destructive coping mechanisms? Once you identify the triggers, then you can give yourself a reality check, or reach out and ask someone who can help you move out of this emotion.

For example, I was talking to a client I will refer to as Danielle. She was getting ready for her wedding, and she went into shame after her mother criticized her appearance. Danielle grew up being physically and emotionally abused by both parents. When other family members witnessed this abuse, Danielle said that they turned their back on her. There were times she said when her mother ridiculed her in front of her grandparents, and she says, "They just stood there and watched. They said nothing."

At her final dress fitting, Danielle told me that her mother walked into the store and said, "That dress does not look flattering on you. I thought you were going to lose more weight before the wedding." When Danielle talked about this incident, she coiled up onto my sofa and began to sob. She asked me what was wrong with her. She wanted me to explain to her, "Why do my parents hate me so much?" She even went on to say, "There must be something wrong with ME if both of my parents do not love me." As we went through the session, I talked with Danielle about intergenerational abuse and how, in this case, it seemed like her parents were passing on similar experiences that they'd had growing up. Danielle's affect brightened slightly as she told me about some memories her mother shared with her about her own mother. She told me that her parents came from abusive families, and that her mother's family was more concerned about appearance than someone's actual happiness.

Danielle struggled a lot with her body image as she became an adolescent. We identified that this was one of her triggers to her shame. As she told me the story, she was able to recognize that her mother was projecting and passing on her own self-hatred. I suggested that she write down some of the positive comments people were giving her as her wedding day was approaching. She told me about her fiancé, and how he was the complete opposite of her mother and father. Danielle said he never commented on her appearance, except to say that he thought she was beautiful, on the inside and out. Danielle recognized that when she talked to her fiancé about belittling comments made by either of her parents, that she was able to plant her feet on the ground and shift into self-care and tend to her hurt self.

For weeks, Danielle and I worked on helping her develop self-kindness and understanding about how she perceived herself. Instead of continuing to blame herself for her parents' limitations, she was able to move into compassion for herself and all the times she felt diminished, abused, and unlovable. The week before Danielle's wedding, we spoke about the negative thoughts and how she could replace those statements with phrases like "The man I am marrying thinks I am beautiful" and "My adulthood is just beginning, and I am proud of the person I am becoming and who I am choosing to spend the rest of my life with."

REPLACING SHAME WITH SELF-COMPASSION

Shame from childhood abuse manifests itself into critical self-talk, self-destructive behaviors, and other forms of self-harm. It causes abuse survivors to develop victim-like behaviors, expecting to be treated poorly by others. Shame leads to a pattern of toxic or abusive relationships. Sadly, according to the Department Health and Human Services, about 30 percent of childhood abuse survivors will go on to abuse their own children as adults.[5]

For most of us, shame is one of the worst effects in the aftermath of abuse. The good news is that there are ways to combat shame so that we can begin to see the world through a different lens. We can find a way to get rid of toxic messages that make us feel inadequate, damaged, worthless, or unlovable. Replacing shame with self-compassion enables us to validate our experiences and no longer accept abusive behaviors done to ourselves or done to us by others. One of the worst parts of childhood abuse is that many of us lived through a variety of harrowing experiences without a compassionate witness. We did not have someone there to help us. We did not have someone that chose to rescue us or remove us from the situation. We did not have someone to help us heal our injuries or give us a hug.

One of the hardest parts of my recovery was sitting with all the pain I felt when I talked about what I called the "day-after memories." Many of us blocked out the actual incidents of abuse, but we remembered what we felt the next day. For example, I remembered many times when I felt pain in my body the day after I was sexually abused. I talked with Dorothy about the longing for a mom. I used to tell her that it was too late. I would yell and scream as I talked about the yearning to have someone tend to my hurt body. Talking about abuse from my childhood, in my thirties, felt like a missed opportunity. There were times when I lashed out at Dorothy for ending the session. I would say things like "So that's it. You are just going to go home and be with your family after everything I just told you." I could not understand why she would not hug me or take care of me. When I spoke about the memories, it felt like the trauma had just happened. I reexperienced the emotions I felt in my body and heart. I wanted to go back to those times and redo the ending of the memory.

Dorothy was not in my life to replace the mother I never had. It was not her job to stop everything she was doing to tend to my wounds. No matter what she said or did, that was not going to change the fact that I felt rejected and unloved by both of my parents. Dorothy was holding a boundary because she was trying to teach me how to honor and love myself. I needed to reframe how I viewed our relationship. I was not unlovable or unworthy of receiving support. I needed to learn how to sit with my grief and move the shame aside as the memories surfaced, instead of allowing that feeling to dictate my perception of myself growing up. I needed to take charge of my inner healing and develop ways to nurture myself. As time went on, I became less angry at Dorothy after speaking about another memory. Instead, I developed a list of tools I would utilize before, during, and after our sessions. When the shame surfaced, I took walks, I reached out to friends, I sat on the beach, I went for hikes, and I listened to music. I pictured my older self wrapping my arms around the five-, ten-, and fifteen-year-old Shari that was so hurt. I began having an internal dialogue, saying things like "Shari, you are lovable. You are strong. You are creating a beautiful life filled with love and light." I wrote in my journal and instead of hurting myself, I went into periods of celebrating my courage for having let myself know and speak about another buried memory.

I worked with one young woman in her mid-twenties—I will refer to her as Kathy—who also grew up feeling parentless. Kathy's mother was angry, hostile, and physically abusive until she left for college at age eighteen. Kathy struggled a lot with peers from her early childhood. She was bullied and sexually harassed for years. She had a dance teacher that belittled and shamed her for being "slightly overweight," and she told me her mother never spoke up and told the dance teacher to stop. Kathy witnessed many incidents when her mother abused her father. She told me she used to hide in her closet when they got into fights. Kathy said that her mother would punch her father and throw things at him. She said her dad stood there, frozen in fear. As Kathy got older, she started recording incidents between her parents. One day she came into session saying, "You've got to listen to this." Kathy played a voice recording of her mother screaming at her father, calling him all kinds of names and throwing glasses, which shattered all over their kitchen.

When I asked Kathy what made her decide to record their fights, she told me, "Because I didn't have a witness, and I wanted my friends or someone to know the kind of house I grew up in." When I began therapy with Kathy, she had little sense of worth or purpose. She was unable to nurture or reassure herself that she was a good person. She went above and beyond to make others happy. If an adult had the slightest look of disapproval, she went into fight-or-flight mode. Kathy told me there were times when she felt like she had an automatic response to people. She explained how her body froze and that words came out of her mouth but that she had no awareness of what was making her say yes in situations when she wanted to say no.

When Kathy got into college, she had some difficult times living with roommates. When we were in therapy, her junior year, she lived with a young woman who was constantly coming home drunk. She told me about one incident when she felt unsafe in her dorm room. Kathy said her roommate was irate and that she was going on and on about something that made her mad. Kathy could feel her body starting to freeze. She watched herself stay silent, instead of telling her roommate to knock it off. One day Kathy told me how she found a place behind her bed where she could go when she felt unsafe. I was touched when she told me, "I felt like the walls were holding me and hugging me." That was the turning point for Kathy. She didn't know this at the time, but that was the first time she went from feeling inadequate and afraid to finding a way to offer herself love and safety. From that point moving forward, Kathy worked on different ways to replicate that feeling of her younger self being held by the mother she wished for while growing up.

As we helped her let go of the shame and understand that we were not the cause of other people's actions as children, we can tend to the part of us that felt helpless, scared, and stranded. Grieving these types of injuries means validating ourselves for our courage and determination to survive unimaginable childhood traumas. When we accept that the abuse was not our fault, we can look back at the child that we once were and take actionable steps to healing through self-care and compassion.

Actionable Steps to Replace Shame with Self-Compassion

- Take a look at Kristin Neff's quotes. This statement sums up how to replace shame with self-compassion. "Painful feelings are, by their very nature, temporary. They will weaken over time as long as we don't prolong or amplify them through resistance or avoidance. The only way to eventually free ourselves from debilitating pain, therefore, is to be with it as it is. The only way out is through."[6]

- Be aware of the shame. As soon as it surfaces, name it. Tell yourselves you will not be a victim of this feeling any longer.

- Replace shame with self-compassion. If someone you loved was suffering, what steps would you take to help that person? Aren't you just as deserving of receiving the love you would give to others in a time of need? The next time you notice feelings of unworthiness or inadequacy, imagine taking your adult self, and have that part talk to your younger self. Talk to your younger self. Speak words of kindness and empathy.

- Accept yourself for who you are. Stop worrying so much about what others think of you. If you catch yourself fearing judgment by others, name that as a projection of your shame. Acknowledge that facing your abuse is painful and extremely difficult. Healing is not about being perfect. Accept your limitations and focus more on your strengths.

- If you feel stuck in shame, talk with someone you trust. Tell that person about some of these crippling thoughts about yourself. Take in the empathy offered by others and keep moving forward.

- Don't let your past define you. Use self-compassion to help you deal with emotions and acknowledge the work you have done to get to this point in your life. Focus on your determination, persistence, and increased awareness about how shame has kept you stuck in the past.

Consider participating in a letter exercise developed by Kristin Neff. This is a powerful exercise that you can share with loved ones or your therapist.

Exploring Self-Compassion through Letter Writing

PART ONE: Everybody has something about themselves that they don't like; something that causes them to feel shame, to feel insecure or not "good enough." It is the human condition to be imperfect, and feelings of failure and inadequacy are part of the experience of living. Try thinking about an issue that tends to make you feel inadequate or bad about yourself (physical appearance, work, or relationship issues, etc.). How does this aspect of yourself make you feel inside—scared, sad, depressed, insecure, angry? What emotions come up for you when you think about this aspect of yourself? Please try to be as emotionally honest as possible and to avoid repressing any feelings, while at the same time not being melodramatic. Try to just feel your emotions exactly as they are—no more, no less.

PART TWO: Now think about an imaginary friend who is unconditionally loving, accepting, kind, and compassionate. Imagine that this friend can see all your strengths and all your weaknesses, including the aspect of yourself you have just been thinking about. Reflect upon what this friend feels toward you, and how you are loved and accepted exactly as you are, with all your very human imperfections. This friend recognizes the limits of human nature and is kind and forgiving toward you. In his/her great wisdom, this friend understands your life history and the millions of things that have happened in your life to create you as you are in this moment. Your particular inadequacy is connected to so many things you didn't necessarily choose: your genes, your family history, life circumstances—things that were outside of your control. Write a letter to yourself from the perspective of this imaginary friend—focusing on the perceived inadequacy you tend to judge yourself for. What would this friend say to you about your "flaw" from the perspective of unlimited compassion? How would this friend convey the deep compassion he/she feels for you, especially for the discomfort you feel when you judge yourself so harshly? What would this friend write in order to remind you that you are only human, that all people have both strengths and weaknesses? And if you think this friend would suggest possible changes you should make, how would these suggestions embody feelings of unconditional understanding and compassion? As you write to yourself from the perspective of this imaginary friend, try to infuse your letter with a strong sense of the person's acceptance, kindness, caring, and desire for your health and happiness. After writing the letter, put it down for a little while. Then come back and read it again, really letting the words sink in. Feel the compassion as it pours into you, soothing and comforting you like a cool breeze on a hot day. Love, connection, and acceptance are your birthright. To claim them you need only look within yourself.[7]

Self-Compassion Statements
Self-compassion statements that you can write, speak, and share with yourself and others! I encourage all of my clients to develop affirmations that they can tell themselves, each and every day, no matter what memory or feeling surfaces. Here are a few of the statements clients have shared with me.

1. I accept myself for who I am.

2. I am so much more than my past.

3. I am not defined by my abuse.

4. I choose to face my trauma and move forward.

5. I choose me!

6. I do not need proof to be heard and believed.

7. I know what happened to me, and I know it was not my fault.

8. I am worthy of feeling love.

9. I can accomplish my dreams.

10. I love the life I am creating.

11. I deserve love and respect.

12. I know there are people in this world that have my back.

13. I have the power to make a difference.

14. Self-compassion helped me survive my childhood.

15. My body is my temple, and no one can tell me otherwise.

CHAPTER 6

Accessing Your Anger

IT IS NORMAL TO BE ANGRY AFTER ABUSE

Childhood abuse leaves us with many side effects, many of which last a lifetime. Anger is the most common response to any type of abuse. Our anger helped us to survive horrific life events as children. In most cases, we were not able to access our rage as the abuse occurred, but that does not mean that the emotion went away. Most of our anger has sat in our bodies and hearts for decades, and we need to find ways to identify and validate our anger.

According to Dr. Hargrove, a clinical psychologist at Duke Health, "When someone experiences childhood trauma, it's often a situation where their power was taken away, or they were not allowed to voice what they felt or what they needed." She goes on to explain that it is appropriate for childhood abuse survivors to have anger as they were put in situations that were very wrong and painful. She explains that anger serves a purpose, and it can be used effectively if we can identify where it is coming from, and we can process the emotion in healthy ways.[1]

Betrayal anger is a type of anger that occurs when people who were supposed to love and protect us violated our trust and our well-being as children. The betrayal trauma theory, created by

Dr. Jennifer Freyd, "posits that there is a social utility in remaining unaware of abuse when the perpetrator is a caregiver. . . . The theory draws on studies of social contracts (e.g., Cosmides, 1989) to explain why and how humans are excellent at detecting betrayals; however, Freyd argues that under some circumstances detecting betrayals may be counter-productive to survival."[2] Examples of betrayal trauma include childhood physical, sexual, and emotional abuse.

The research on anger and adult survivors of childhood abuse suggests that it may not surface until later in life, because the anger is masked by feelings of shame and secrecy.[3] Abused children do not feel safe expressing their emotions, especially anger.

One study, talked about in Catherine Riessman's book *Narrative Methods for Human Sciences*, explored five types of anger that survivors of abuse often report as adults.[4]

1. **Self-castigating anger**: This type of anger involves beating ourselves up if we do or did anything wrong. Many of my clients beat themselves up and call themselves derogatory names, such as stupid or dumb. For example, one of my clients, whom I will refer to as Ann, was angry at herself for not confronting her boyfriend, who often berated her in public. She told me on several occasions, "I am such a coward. I just sit there and let him humiliate me." Ann would freeze when she sensed the slightest bit of disapproval, but she would also tell me that she felt like her insides were burning up. She felt anger, but she was unable to express her feelings or set a boundary. Instead, Ann blamed herself for other people's poor choices.

2. **Displaced anger**: This type of anger is directed at people who are not the source of the problem. For example, if you find yourself losing your temper with your children, you may be placing anger you felt at your own parents onto your

children, because they are not being hurt, the way you were when you were children. I worked with one client—I will call him Michael—who lost his temper quite often in public. He described being an impatient customer and he also talked about his reaction to traffic when he was on his way to work. One time, I heard him screaming at the cars in front of him as he pulled over, so he could talk to me on a videocall, because traffic prevented him from arriving at my office for our session. His face turned bright red as expletives were coming out of his mouth. Initially, he was embarrassed that I witnessed this response. However, we were able to talk about what feelings got activated when he realized he would not make it to my office for our therapy session. He realized that he was displacing his anger onto strangers in cars because he felt trapped and held up. Being stuck in traffic reminded him of times when he was locked in his bedroom, with his abusive father, who would lash out onto him, when no one else was home. Once Michael was able to understand the root of his anger, he was able to release his shame and better manage unavoidable circumstances, which he had no control over.

3. **Anger of Indignation**: This type of anger comes from the realization that we are people who do not deserve to be mistreated by others. For many of us, this revelation can happen suddenly, like a switch in our brain suddenly turns on. I have worked with several clients who have come to understand that they do not and did not deserve to be abused. Oftentimes, it is a turning point that happens in an unhealthy adult relationship with a family member, boss, or partner. It is an empowering moment when clients can tell themselves, "I do not deserve to be abused." I remember dozens of times as a child thinking, "I will show you." The anger I felt helped me to keep fighting and utilize that energy as an adult to take back my life as an adult.

4. **Self-protective anger:** This type of anger is a result of having no protection as children. Many of us needed our anger to protect our integrity. I have worked with several clients who have abusive partners as adults. Self-protective anger allows us to set boundaries and say no more. I worked with one woman in her thirties, whom I will refer to as Miranda. She started dating another woman years after facing abuse done to her by a church member and her mother. Part of her healing was about reclaiming her right to be angry at her mother for allowing members of the church into her childhood home. At times she was angrier at her mother for enabling the abuse, rather than the perpetrator itself. She met a woman with whom she began to fall in love. However, red flags started to surface as they spent more time together. I will never forget the day Miranda announced in session, "I am going to call this woman out on her shit rather than allow her to belittle me and make me feel like a horrible person." She realized that she was accessing buried anger she had never expressed to her mother growing up. Miranda stepped in as an adult and found a way to protect the part of herself that felt abandoned as a child.

5. **Righteous anger on behalf of self or others:** This type of anger stirs up the injustice we feel toward our perpetrators. As we grow into adulthood and we understand the impact of the abuse, we get in touch with the enormous harm that was put on us by others. I remember talking in therapy about my parents and saying things like "They are out here living great lives, serving no jail time or paying for all the harm they caused me." While anger can stir up feelings of helplessness, it is healthy to hold our perpetrators accountable. It is normal to feel angry about all the work we need to do to heal, because of other people's crazy choices and behaviors. This type of anger often propels us to advocate for ourselves

and others. There are thousands of survivors volunteering and trying to change laws for children of the future.

DEFINING EMOTIONS CONNECTED TO ANGER

Dealing with emotions connected to our anger helps us release the feeling and better protect ourselves in relationships with others. A key question to consider is where is your anger coming from? Often, there are more personalized emotions that lay beneath the anger that gets triggered in the present. For example, many of us may experience feelings of shame when we start to feel angry. If we think someone is disapproving of something we said or did, our first instinct is to shrink up and feel "bad" or "wrong."

Anger is often a secondary emotion, masking feelings such as fear or sadness. Fear includes anxiety and worry, and sadness comes from experiencing loss or disappointment. Feeling fear and sadness is uncomfortable because it makes us feel vulnerable or even out of control. Many of us shift subconsciously into anger because it makes us feel more in control, rather than helpless. When anger arises between couples, oftentimes there's a fear of abandonment or rejection underneath.

I was in therapy with a woman in her forties, whom I will refer to as Michelle, who had an extensive childhood abuse history. Her mother emotionally abused her, and she was sexually abused multiple times by a neighbor that lived three doors down from her childhood home. As she progressed in her healing, she allowed herself to have more of the things that she wanted. She was terrified of having children because she assumed she would be just like her mother. She was afraid she would not be able to protect a child from being abused by an adult.

When I met Michelle, she was forty-two years old. She was a huge animal lover. She spent years riding horses and volunteering at an animal shelter walking dogs. A year after we started therapy, Michelle rescued a three-year-old dog. Nuggs, Michelle's dog, was abused for the first year of her life. She lived in unsafe and unsanitary conditions. Michelle had wanted a dog of her own since she was in her twenties. When she met Nuggs, she told me something switched in her brain and she felt ready to be a dog owner. Michelle developed a nurturing, safe relationship with her dog. She took Nuggs on hikes and road trips in her minivan. About a year after she rescued her dog, she began dating a man named Ken.

It took months for Michelle to feel comfortable bringing Nuggs with her when she spent the night with Ken. We had a session the week after Ken met her dog. Michelle was triggered because she said Ken was standoffish with her dog, and she assumed it was because of something she or her dog was doing. We talked about how to help Michelle talk with Ken about her feelings and how to handle the situation.

Nuggs was part of her life and Michelle was not willing to let another person get in the way of their connection. Over the next few months, Michelle told me that Ken was more accepting of her dog. He had pets living in his home too, two cats and a dog. Michelle told me Ken was protective of his pet family. Michelle understood that feeling, and she was determined to find a way to accept his feelings while setting her own boundaries.

About six months later Michelle told me that Nuggs had a bad moment. She growled at Ken after he tried to hug Michelle. Michelle sobbed as she told me what happened next. She said that Ken's first reaction was to tell Michelle that she needed to train her dog. Michelle said she felt her insides boiling as he went on a rant about how to parent a dog. She told me, "I went back to many times in my life as a kid when I felt like a piece of shit when my mom ridiculed me." As the session continued Michelle's voice softened, and she kept saying, "I am such a bad person." However, about five minutes after the shame surfaced, Michelle's tone switched. I asked her how she felt about Ken's feedback and delivery of his message. She paused for a second and then she said, "Wait a minute, he is trying to make me feel like I did something wrong and that if I do not fix whatever is bothering him, he will leave." Then Michelle accessed her anger.

She talked about several other incidents with Nuggs when she was given instructions by Ken about his house rules and that she obliged, rather than compromise. We talked about Michelle's response to Ken's rules, and she realized she was accommodating and trying to push away her anger. I asked her if you were not feeling afraid, what would you be feeling? Michelle got in touch with her anger. She made the connection between feeling angry and feeling hurt and afraid. She realized that Ken had hurt her feelings, as she loved her dog, and she did not feel like Ken was accepting of that. She realized that she was having a similar response to Ken as she did when she was growing up with her mother. As Michelle got more in touch with how she masked her anger as a child, we developed different strategies she could use to hold her anger and express it appropriately.

Actionable Steps to Defining Emotions Connected to Your Anger

- Do you stuff your anger down and then take it out on yourself?
- Do you lash out at others and feel angry all the time?
- Do you try and numb out by smoking, eating, or drinking alcohol?
- Do you have alternatives you could turn to if you answered yes to any of the questions above?
- If you feel triggered and you cannot access your anger, speak out. Call a friend. Write in your journal.
- Instead of telling yourself that you are bad for feeling angry, affirm yourself for naming the feeling.
- Write statements on a piece of paper. "I am allowed to be angry." "It is okay to feel mad." "Feeling angry does not make me a bad person." "Anger is a normal emotion." "My

anger cannot hurt myself or others, unless I allow that to happen."

- Instead of beating yourself up, do something nice for yourself. Comfort the part of you that felt beaten up or shamed when others took their anger out on you!

- Give yourself permission to cry. Releasing anger can come out in the form of tears. It helps to get rid of all your frustration.

- Play loud, angry music. Sit in your body and recognize that this is a normal emotion or there would not be music with angry themes in it!

- Do some writing in your journal or diary. Freely express your anger. Talk to yourself in your writing. Affirm and acknowledge the feeling. Remind yourself of the courage it takes to own your anger.

When to Seek Help to Manage Your Anger

- You cannot keep yourself safe when you are angry. You may have the urge to use self-destructive vices such as disordered eating, substance abuse, or self-harm.

- You act on your anger in ways that you regret afterward.

- You hurt people around you to show them you are angry.

- Your anger consumes you.

- You start fights with coworkers, friends, and/or partners.

- You become violent when you are angry.

- You have an urge to act violently toward yourself or others.

POWER OF USING ANGER TO CREATE CHANGE

Anger is not a destructive emotion, rather it is an empowering feeling that can help us cope with our trauma. Anger helped us to identify that something was not right and that we were not being treated with kindness or in an appropriate way. It motivates us to make changes and it allows us to keep moving forward. When we felt threatened growing up, the anger helped us protect ourselves. Most of us experienced the fight-or-flight response when anger was being expressed through violence or aggression. Adults who grew up in families where anger was modeled in a proper way were able to learn how to recognize their anger and deal with it.

There is a book written by Pete Walker, who writes about grieving the losses of childhood that come from growing up in a dysfunctional family system. He focuses on four practices of grieving that must be done in trauma therapy. Walker talks about "angering, crying, verbal ventilating and feeling."[5] Walker defines angering as "expressing one's feelings of resentment and rage over the trauma inflicted by an abuser in a way that does not hurt either the survivor or anyone else." He goes on to explain that angering is a grieving strategy of voicing current or past losses and injustices.

As we move forward in our healing process, we need a safe space and a safe way to talk about the rage associated with humiliation, neglect, and lack of safety growing up. That does not mean that we need to confront the perpetrator directly. As we get in touch with our rage about the abuse, we need to redirect the anger that we have internalized and then comes out in the form of a malicious inner critic. For example, if you are saying things to yourself like "I brought the abuse on myself" or "I should have been able to stop it," you want to respond to these messages saying things like "No, I was just a child and I did not have the power to stop the abuse or neglect." Standing up to our inner critic allows us to place the anger and blame where it belongs. "Angering is therapeutic when the survivor rails against childhood trauma, and especially when she rails against its living continuance in the self-hate processes of the critic."[6] Angrily fighting off the inner critic by shouting, "No! You cannot talk to me that way!" stops the survivor from turning anger toward themselves, and therefore rescues the survivor from toxic shame and a childlike sense of powerlessness. Standing up to the inner critic (i.e., the internalized abuser) helps survivors redirect blame to where it belongs and set up the healthy ego function of self-protection.

Using our anger in productive, healthy ways allows us to decrease repetitive episodes of being bullied or mistreated. Walker also talks about the importance of crying to release the pain of abandonment that we felt in childhood. I have seen dozens of clients who have learned to access their anger, and often find that the first step to feeling it is speaking about it directly and then finding ways to let it out. There were hundreds of times when I sat in session with my therapist, and I sobbed as I came to terms with all that was lost in my childhood. Once I was able to recognize how hurt I felt and not blame myself, I was able to feel the rage and express it toward my parents with my therapist. There were times when I would feel like it was pointless to tell Dorothy how bad I felt. However, I noticed that when I owned my anger and released it, I was able to then go out in the world and seek out goals and dreams in my personal and professional life.

While it may seem impossible to work through repressed anger, it is not! There are strategies we can use to express our anger in a productive way, rather than stuffing the feelings into our bodies and minds. Developing skills to name our anger, where it is coming from, and releasing it allows us to feel more connected to other people. Expressing our anger allows us to be more assertive and to get our needs met.

Actionable Steps to Releasing Anger

- Name the emotion when you are feeling angry.
- Remove yourself from the situation if you need a minute to process your feelings.
- Consider practicing mindfulness or meditation to cope with the intensity of the emotion.

- Use physical activity or exercise to release suppressed or pent-up rage.
- Get at least eight hours of sleep each night.
- Journal about your feelings.
- Get a dog or a service animal.
- Be present with your anger. Focus on staying grounded so you can find underlying issues that need your attention.
- Express your anger differently than you have in the past. For example, if your tendency is to scream or throw things when you are mad, try writing or punching a soft pillow instead.
- If you notice your heart rate goes up or that your body is responding to your anger in ways that make you feel scared or uncomfortable, practice relaxation and breathing strategies.
- Move forward with compassion and kindness. Remind yourself that anger is a human emotion and that we all feel it at times. We are not our abusers if we feel rage or inadvertently take it out onto someone else. We are in the healing process and working toward owning our anger and then finding ways to release it appropriately. Learn from past mistakes. Be grateful that you can access your anger rather than shame yourself for feeling angry.
- Visualize your anger dissipating after you express it. Take a few minutes to sit with the feeling and then imagine letting it go. Imagine the anger leaving your body and being able to focus on the relief you will feel after you express it.

Another concept Pete Walker emphasizes in his work is the concept of forgiveness.[7] Most of my clients struggle with using their anger because they want to protect the people that have caused them harm. It is not uncommon for clients to tell me that they have never been able to use their anger to create change. In fact, most of the survivors I have met are quick to forgive their perpetrators, which then results in them pushing their anger down further.

There are many reasons why we might want to jump to forgiveness. Have you heard yourself saying things like "I don't want to rock the boat" or "Why dredge up the past?" Through the years have you had bystanders or other family members or friends tell you that if you stay mad you are hurting other people? These messages are internalized, and then we feel like bad people for wanting to hold our abusers accountable. Our inner critic holds us back from working through the anger. We may feel like we should just "get over it," or that we will get hurt if we express the anger onto the people that hurt us. Most of us picked up unhealthy messages about feeling angry and that holds us back from moving into a place of compassion or forgiveness.

For example, I was working with one woman, whom I will refer to as Alex. She started seeing me because she had developed bulimia a couple of years after she left for college. Alex was sexually abused by her older brother during her childhood. A few months after she left for college, she confronted her parents about the abuse. She wanted to know why they did not notice that he was hurting her. Alex told me that her parents got incredibly angry at her and that they said she was "ruining their lives" by making such claims.

When I met Alex, her eating disorder was out of control. She was bingeing and purging multiple times a day. Within a few months of meeting with me, Alex realized that she was using bulimia as a way to get rid of her anger, without having to speak the feelings aloud. She gained insight into the role of her eating disorder, and then she was able to find other ways to manage those self-destructive urges. Alex told me that after she confronted her parents about the abuse, her eating disorder got worse. In our therapy sessions, we talked at length about her parents' response and what that meant to her. Alex blamed herself for the abuse for years, but once she got to college, she realized that her brother hurt her and that her parents did not protect her. It took Alex months to come to terms with their denial and inability to be a part of her healing process.

When Alex was getting ready to graduate college, she moved into a place of acceptance. She spent months coming to terms with the fact that she was going to have to work through her abuse without the support of her family. She recognized that healing for her meant walking on a different path than the one she imagined once she decided to break her silence. Alex looked closer at her parents' childhoods, and the intergenerational abuse that went back to her great grandparents. While Alex's parents were very closed off about sharing more about their childhoods, she was able to put pieces of the puzzle together by talking to other family members. Alex's cousin told her that her mother and Alex's mother were sexually abused by their father growing up. Another family member on her father's side told her that her dad saw domestic violence between his mother and father.

Alex gave herself time to be with her anger during her healing journey. She realized that holding onto her eating disorder and pushing her anger away was not going to allow her to live the life she wanted. At one point Alex wrote a letter to her eating disorder. One of the questions she asked herself was "What am I trying to stuff down and get rid of when I use my symptoms of bulimia?" Alex learned through her therapy and a lot of soul searching that she was going to need to accept her past without the support and acknowledgment of her family. She had a choice: continue burying her anger or find ways to cope with her feelings and move into a place of acceptance. Over time, Alex replaced her eating disorder symptoms with yoga, mindfulness, and pet therapy.

Alex came to terms with the pathology of her abuser and her parents. She knew her brother was in pain and that he had severe emotional problems. She accepted that her parents could not let themselves see the truth because of their own abusive childhood, which she assumed they never dealt with. Instead of feeling compassion for her brother and her parents, Alex felt empathy for her brother and the choices he made. She put herself in her parents' shoes and affirmed herself for knowing her parents could have heard her and protected her if they had dealt with their earlier childhood trauma. Alex used her anger by giving herself permission to keep distance from her family and deciding that she was going to break generations of abuse within her nuclear family.

Some questions we can consider as we confront our anger about the abuse: How do we find a way to forgive people who never take responsibility for what they have done to us? How do we continue to use our anger to create change and break the cycle of abuse and abandonment in our adulthoods? How do we forgive others while keeping our boundaries and staying the truth?

1. Remember that forgiving your abuser does not mean that you need to have that person in your life!

2. Forgiveness does not mean that we need to reconcile. We do not need to discuss our abuse with people who refuse to accept the truth. We can forgive our abusers without allowing them to be involved in that process.

3. Forgiveness does not mean that we need to change our boundaries. We can decide what boundaries we need to keep ourselves safe, and we can decide what we will and won't tolerate.

4. Forgiveness does not mean that we "get over" what happened to us. Forgiving our abusers is a process, and it can take years. Many times, we will slip and slide in this part of our journey. One day we may think what happened was not that bad. On another day we may realize that the abuse was awful. Forgiveness is not a straight line, rather it can be

bumpy and confusing. As we evolve into adulthood and create a life for ourselves, we may long for our abusers, because we did love them and now may want them to be a part of our accomplishments and dreams.

5. Forgiveness does not mean that we then can trust our abusers. We get to decide if it is safe to try and rebuild trust with people that have caused us harm in our childhoods.

CHAPTER 7

Drawing Boundaries

HOLDING THE LINE

Our boundaries were largely formed in our childhoods. If our needs had been met appropriately, and we felt safe and secure in our earlier years, we would have an idea of healthy boundaries. Many of us were robbed of our sense of safety from the abuse we survived in childhood.

There are many different types of boundary infractions. If you grew up in a family and suffered sexual abuse by a trusted adult, you may have felt out of control in your own body. You were given the message from a young age that you do not have a say in how others view or treat the body that you lived in. If you grew up in a home with emotional and physical abuse, most likely you were not taught how to communicate when you felt like your emotional boundaries were disrespected.

There are different kinds of boundaries that may have been violated in our childhoods. Physical boundaries include our bodies, personal space, and privacy. An example of a physical boundary violation is when someone hits us, or violates our personal space, by coming into our bathroom or bedroom without asking permission. Another example of a physical boundary violation is when a trusted adult touches us inappropriately or engages in unwanted sexual acts with us. Other examples of physical boundary violations are looking through our phones or emails or barging into our bedrooms when we are getting undressed.

Emotional boundaries are set up to protect our sense of self and allow us to separate our feelings from others. An example of an emotional boundary infraction is when adults looked to us, as children, as the mediator or protector. Another example is when we were made to feel at fault for things that were not our responsibility. It is not uncommon in families where abuse occurs for one of the adults to enable or become a silent bystander to the other adults who are causing harm. I have worked with dozens of clients who have felt emotionally neglected by their parents or trusted adults when they tried to tell them about the abuse being done to them. Many of my clients have reported feeling disbelieved and diminished when they tried to tell someone that they were being abused or mistreated.

When I started therapy with Dorothy in my mid-twenties, I had never heard of the word boundaries. Very early in our work together, she asked me what kind of boundaries my parents had with me when I was growing up. I just looked at her, perplexed. When she used that word, I felt ashamed. I could not identify where the shame was coming from, and I did not understand why I felt like my body was being violated when that subject came up in session. I did not understand how my silence was my way of having boundaries in a system where there were no boundaries.

Throughout the years I have gained much more insight into the importance of boundaries and the impact of having to depend on untrustworthy adults to survive. It took me years to understand my attachment style and where that came from. In therapy, I explored relationships with adults that were in my life during childhood. I talked to Dorothy about how I formed unrealistic connections with women. I sought out loving, reliable mother figures, not realizing I was trying to find an adult that would love me or rescue me from my family. I also spent hours talking with

Dorothy about my tendency to go into fight or freeze mode with my father and many other male adult connections. At the time I did not understand that I was trying to protect myself and feel some sense of stability with the few adults I did trust growing up.

Janina Fisher, author of *Healing the Fragmented Selves of Trauma Survivors*, used childhood research to explain how survivors of abuse dealt with boundary violations growing up. Fisher explains that "[w]hen attachment figures are abusive, the child's only source of safety and protection simultaneously becomes the source of immediate danger, leaving the child caught between two conflicting sets of instincts. On the one hand, they are driven by the attachment instinct to seek proximity, comfort, and protection from attachment figures. On the other, they are driven by equally strong animal defense instincts to freeze, fight, flee or submit . . . before they get too close to the frightening parent."[1]

In other words, Fisher explains that as children we formed a strong bond with our abuser so we could survive. The relationship is complex because on one hand we are terrified of abusive adults, but many of us also needed to depend on these same people to survive. In order to heal and reestablish safety with ourselves and others, we need to evaluate the coping mechanisms we used from childhood and then decide which ones to keep and which ones no longer serve us. We need to look back at the fundamental aspects of our development that were impeded by those adults that caused us harm.

As you look back on your childhood and gain awareness of your boundaries in adulthood, do you notice how you wear a mask to keep people at arm's length. For example, do you say, "I am fine" even when you are not? Do you say it is okay, even when it is not okay? Are you agreeable, low-maintenance, and pleasant to be around? Do you work harder than is necessary to make others feel comfortable? Do you put the needs of others ahead of yourself? Is it hard for you to plan when it involves other people? Are you unable to ask for what you need? Do you struggle with saying no?

Do you blame yourself when others seem angry or sad? Do you worry too much about what others are thinking?

I was working with one woman in her early thirties—let's call her Marcy. She was in a serious relationship with another woman whom I will call Kathy. Marcy had a history of abuse done to her by her older sister. She spent a few years in therapy talking about the lack of boundaries in her household. Marcy told me her dad was oblivious to the abuse and that her mom enabled the sister's controlling and at times physically abusive behavior. Marcy struggled extensively with setting boundaries. In therapy we talked about the fight-or-flight response and how it was triggered when she felt Kathy was disapproving of something that Marcy said or did. They had several arguments about Marcy's dog, who Kathy felt was an intrusion in the relationship. One time when I met with Marcy, I noticed that she began dissociating as she talked to me about a fight they had just had the night before our session.

Marcy said that she and Kathy were talking about living together. As they moved closer to making those arrangements, Kathy told Marcy, "I want to live with you, but I do not like your dog." Marcy's voice shook as she told me the story. When I asked her if the feelings that were getting activated with Kathy felt familiar, she said it reminded her of times when her older sister pinned her down and made her do things she did not want to do! During her childhood, Marcy gave in to her sister's requests, even though she wanted to say no.

Marcy and I talked about her relationship with Kathy and how the boundaries in that relationship mimicked some of the patterns with her older sister. In one session, Marcy broke down in tears as she talked about how she felt like she had to choose between her dog or staying with Kathy.

Figuring out what is tolerable or manageable versus deciding that certain things are off the table is an important part of holding the line in relationships. Marcy came back into therapy the next week, and she told me that she had decided being with a partner that could not or would not accept her dog was not going to work for her. Marcy told me she'd had several conversations with Kathy, trying to come up with a plan that would work for both of them. Marcy realized that Kathy was rigid and controlling and unwilling to budge when it came to what she wanted. While this was a painful decision for Marcy, it was the choice that she needed to make. Marcy did not want to continue staying in relationships where she had to drop her boundary to make the other person happy.

Establishing healthy boundaries is healing and empowering. By recognizing the importance of setting limits, we can protect our sense of self and worth and engage in healthy relationships. If we continue to put our wants and needs aside, we are at much more risk of developing dependency, depression, and anxiety. We need to be able to speak up when other people are acting in ways that are not acceptable. As adults, it is our responsibility to decide how we allow others to treat us. We need to learn examples of healthy behaviors when interacting with others. We need to be honest with ourselves and our feelings when we feel like our boundaries are being crossed. We need to learn how to be direct and honest when we are communicating with others when we are setting boundaries. We need to find ways to overcome the fear of rejection or loss if others cannot respect our boundaries.

Learning how to communicate without using blame is an integral part of the process. Many of us grew up hearing people telling us or others, "You did this," or "It is your fault that I hit you." We need to learn how to place ownership on others, by saying things like "I feel angry when you talk down to me" or "I am not okay with being belittled by you when I make a mistake."

In order to establish healthy boundaries, we need to know the warning signs that we are lacking in setting those limits. Here are some questions you may want to ask yourself:

1. Am I "people pleasing"?

2. Am I feeling burned out or overextended?

3. Am I putting other people's needs ahead of my own?

4. In order to receive from others, do I give to the extreme, without considering myself or my well-being?

5. Am I sharing too much too soon? Am I closing myself off and not expressing any of my needs or wants?

6. Do I feel responsible for other people's happiness?

7. Do I stop myself from saying no because I am afraid of being rejected or abandoned?

8. Do I base how I feel about myself on how others treat me?

9. Do I allow others to make decisions for me, even if my intuition is telling me not to do that?

I worked with one woman in her early twenties whom I will refer to as Katie. I met her in her junior year of high school. Her mother reached out to me saying Katie had depression and anxiety. Once I met Katie, her mother had very little involvement in our therapy. At one point she told me that she had been sexually assaulted by her therapist growing up and that she did not trust therapists. Over time I talked with Katie about how she felt about her mother's lack of involvement in her mental health treatment. I will never forget the time when Katie walked into my office sobbing. Katie opened up about an emotional barrage her mother went on about Katie's appearance. She told me, "My mother hates everything about me. She doesn't like my hair. She tells me to lose weight. And she often says no one will ever be attracted to me."

Once I realized that her mother was emotionally unavailable and seemed to have several narcissistic qualities, I focused on helping Katie set boundaries. There were times when saying no was impossible because Katie would tell me if she did not do what her mother said that she would kick her out of the house. At the end of her senior year of high school, Katie had a plan. She received a full scholarship to a college hundreds of miles away from her family. By that point Katie's dad had taken a job that required him to live separately from her and her mother.

Katie continued to see me in therapy once she started college. She was thriving but still struggling to manage her relationship with her mother. Katie told me her mother tracked her phone and that she demanded to know her grades. Early in the fall semester, Katie developed some autoimmune health issues. Her primary doctor suggested she see two different specialists to diagnose and treat the disorders. Katie came to session one week having what she called a total "meltdown." She was sobbing and could barely speak as she told me what her primary doctor recommended. Katie told me her mother would not let her see these specialists and that she was just saying she had issues to get attention. Together, we tried to figure out a way for Katie to get what she needed and set boundaries with her mother.

I talked to Katie about taking over her medical care, as she was over eighteen and she had the financial means to pay for doctor's visits. At first Katie was terrified that if she defied her mother, she would force Katie to leave college. We talked about her fears and how they were certainly appropriate given her history. We also talked about the choices she had moving forward now that she was a legal adult.

It took Katie a few months to move forward with making these doctor appointments. Katie spent her whole life feeling afraid and expendable. She knew her mother's demands and expectations were inappropriate. Katie had to gain trust in herself and that if her mother walked out of her life that she would be okay. With determination and courage Katie set some boundaries. She stopped letting her mother track her phone. She stopped texting her grades when she took tests or handed in papers. She ended phone calls with her mother when she criticized Katie's appearance or commented on her weight. Katie made appointments to see the specialists, and she was able to get the help she needed. Once Katie found her voice, she was able to gain insight into her mother's pathology. She realized that her mother's behaviors were caused by pathology that had nothing to do with her. Katie found ways to communicate with her mother and do the things she needed to do to take care of herself. She realized she did not need to tell her mother everything that was going on in her life. She made choices, and instead of trying to get her mother's approval, she would move forward if she approved of the decisions she was trying to make.

Actionable Steps to Holding the Line and Setting Boundaries

- Identify the boundaries you want to set. Learn how to give yourself approval rather than seek that from others.

- Accept that others may be disappointed with your boundaries. People may try to make you feel guilty for setting a limit. Create a plan on how to deal with the guilt if that is what you are left with.

- Be mindful of what you share with others. You do not need to confide in people or share details about anything in your life, no matter what the relationship is. It is okay to filter out what you share and to decide who you share with.

- If people begin to argue with you or try to talk you out of a decision, do not engage. Hold your line and keep your feet planted on why you created that boundary.

- Reduce the amount of time you spend with people that have hurt you in the past. Engage in activities that involve other people or in public places. Have an exit strategy. Decide before you go how long you want to stay. Be clear about the amount of time you have to spend with those people before you arrive. For example, you can say you need to leave by this time to pick up a child from school or be home to start cooking dinner.

- Put yourself first. Make self-care your priority. Make time for therapy, exercise, meditation, time outdoors, reading, or spending time with the people with whom you feel safe. The more you take care of yourself, the less you will accept toxicity from others.

- Come to terms with the pathology of the people that hurt you. That will give you the strength to hold your line and continue to set boundaries moving forward.

USING YOUR VOICE AND QUIETING THE GUILT

What steps can we take to establish healthy boundaries? The first and most important step to attaining this goal is we need to find our voices. As we saw in Katie's story, once she realized the pathology of her mother and how to manage it, she needed to use her voice to assert her boundaries.

Once we find our voices, boundaries may continue to be difficult because the abuse taught us that if we say no, we put ourselves at risk of getting hurt or abandoned. Think about times in your adulthood when you wanted to put your foot down and set a limit. What kinds of feelings came up in your body and what kind of thoughts did you have as you tried to use your voice?

I can think of hundreds of times throughout my adulthood when I knew what I needed to do to take care of myself, but then I ended up silencing myself because of the guilt and fear. I have had times when I could feel my body freezing up, my heart racing, and my head pounding when I needed to assert myself. As I go through my healing process, I have been able to recognize the guilt and place it back in the past. I have learned to challenge my self-doubt and accept that I may disappoint others. I have realized that it is not my job to please others, at my own expense. For years I used to tell Dorothy, "I am a horrible daughter." As I distanced myself from family members who refused to take ownership of the abuse, I placed the blame on myself rather than holding them accountable. I felt like I had to put everyone else's needs ahead of my own, even with the people that abused and abandoned my need for protection.

Over time, I have reframed how I approach boundaries and I have accepted that I may always feel guilty for speaking up. Rather than allow guilt to consume me, I place the feeling and I give myself the choice to not allow this emotion to dictate my needs with others.

Recently, I was working with a woman in her thirties; I will refer to her as Stacy. When I met Stacy, she told me that her mother abandoned her and her father when she was seven years old. She said, "I came home from school one day and my mother was gone." Stacy said that she grew up without her mother and that she always blamed herself for her mother's absence. Stacy told me that her mother resurfaced and started making contact when her mother was diagnosed with breast cancer. During that time Stacy was not in counseling, and she felt like she needed to do what her mother asked of her.

Stacy's mother moved into her home with her husband when she was receiving chemotherapy and undergoing surgery for her cancer. Stacy said that their relationship continued to feel strained, and she did not feel like she had the option to consider her needs or feelings about the shift in the boundaries. About a year after her mother completed her cancer treatment, she moved out of Stacy's house and resumed her life, showing very little interest in Stacy or what was going on in her life.

Stacy decided to start therapy after she underwent over a year of infertility treatments. When we started therapy, Stacy told me that her mother showed no interest in her difficulty conceiving. About two months after I met Stacy, she had a miscarriage. She texted her mother about the loss, and the response she got back from her mother via text was "I hope you feel better." Months went by and Stacy restarted infertility treatments. During that time her mother made no contact and showed no interest in Stacy's life. Thankfully, Stacy got pregnant after spending months working with a fertility doctor. She gave birth to a beautiful baby girl. Throughout the pregnancy, Stacy and I spoke about her mother's absence and how she wanted to handle contact with her mother if she showed interest in the baby's life once she was born. There were sessions when Stacy was pregnant and she sobbed in therapy, saying things like "How can my mom be so cold?"

Once the baby was born, Stacy felt obligated to tell her mother about her birth. A few weeks after Stacy's baby was born, we had a session. With pain all over her face, Stacy told me that her mother texted congratulations after the birth of her daughter. She went on to tell me that her mother did not visit or send any items for the baby. The saddest part of all is that Stacy still felt obligated to "fix" things with her mother.

A light bulb went off in Stacy when we talked about where those feelings of guilt came from. She talked about another family member who tried to induce guilt in Stacy by saying, "I really wished you would fix things with your mother." Stacy was able to access her anger and talk about how that comment made her feel. We talked about Stacy's sense of obligation to be there for her mother, no matter how many times she abandoned Stacy growing up or during the miscarriage and the pregnancy. Stacy said to me, "Wait, why am I feeling guilty when my mother has not parented or supported me through the years?"

Stacy found her voice. She accepted that she would need to continue working on containing the guilt when she wanted to set a limit with her mother or other family members who were pressuring her to "fix" things. Once Stacy became a mother herself, her perspective on her responsibilities shifted. She was no longer just someone's daughter; she was also a mother who wanted to create a safe environment for her precious newborn. Stacy worked on her low self-esteem and ways to reframe her reaction with her decision to speak up and set limits when others tried to make her feel bad for the estrangement with her mother. We talked about how becoming a mother herself could help her shift her focus to the family she was creating for herself in her adulthood.

Actionable Steps to Using Your Voice and Quieting the Guilt

- Change the story you are telling yourself when you want or need to say no to others. Instead of judging your boundaries, work on accepting them. Instead of telling yourself, "I feel so guilty about setting that boundary with my dad about visiting him on his birthday," tell yourself, "It is never wrong to listen to my body and follow my intuition about how to keep myself safe." Talk in therapy or with friends about guilt and how recognizing that feeling has given you the opportunity to make better choices moving forward.

- Notice how you feel when you put yourself ahead of others. Do you feel relieved? Do you feel safer? Think about how you are breaking lifelong patterns and how you are no longer allowing others to violate your space or right to say no.

- Talk about the long-term benefits of being aware of your guilt. What messages are you sending to others when you speak up. Are you helping others recognize how their behavior makes you feel uncomfortable? Are you making space to have healthier relationships when you speak up instead of avoiding or talking yourself out of setting a boundary?

- Will you have less resentment for the people you choose to have in your lives as adults if you stop trying to please everyone around you?

- Reframe how you think of boundaries. In the past, have you felt like you had to lie or mislead others to give them what they want? By setting boundaries, you are rewriting an old script that has been repeated for years. You are breaking patterns of self-sacrifice and resentment.

- Talk about or write about why you are setting boundaries. Some examples of "why" are "I am setting boundaries to live a more truthful life." "I am setting limits to show my children how to advocate for themselves or others." "I am developing relationships that are built on authenticity, honesty, and good communication."

- After you decide why you are setting boundaries, consider writing these statements down and sticking them on your refrigerator, bathroom mirror, or even your phone background. Remind yourself that developing healthy boundaries is a process that takes time. Do not beat yourself up if or when you slip, slide, or regress back into old patterns.

CHAPTER 8

Guiding Loved Ones

BECOMING A WITNESS

Many studies have found that adults do not disclose their history of childhood abuse for at least twenty years. In 2020, one study focused on the barriers to speaking out and found that survivors wait at least seventeen years to tell someone what happened to them.[1] One barrier to breaking the silence is that most survivors doubt themselves and their memories.

If we wished for something not to be so, then that thought forces us to stay silent and to live our lives without having a witness. Saying it out loud, "I was abused by my mother or father or sibling or teacher," destroys any hope that we had a "normal" childhood.

How do we allow ourselves to hold the truth and then begin to share our childhood traumas with others? How can our loved ones, therapists, or others in our support system be a witness? How can we help our witnesses understand the impact of childhood abuse?

The first step to becoming a witness is allowing ourselves to understand the ramifications of childhood abuse and the various ways it affects us physically, emotionally, and mentally. One of the most important things you can do for someone else who was abused as a child is to listen without judgment. Let them share their story at their own pace and try not to jump in and ask questions until they have finished speaking. Remind your loved one that they deserve love and support and that you know the abuse was not their fault.

Accounts of childhood abuse are often met with disbelief, because no one wants to think that an adult can inflict these types of harm onto children. It is normal to be skeptical about what you are hearing. Survivors need to know that they are believed. As your loved one shares their truth, try and remind yourself that unimaginable accounts of abuse are possible. There are some very sick people in this world who inflict hurt onto their children. You may have questions in your mind, such as "Why didn't you tell someone?" While these are normal thoughts to have, it is best not to share any thoughts that could leave your loved one feeling unsupported or judged.

Creating a safe and supportive environment is crucial, especially if you want to be a witness and support your loved one on their healing journey. Part of how you can create safety is to remind your loved one that there is no timeline on how much to share. If you sense that your loved one is getting overwhelmed, encourage your loved one to slow down and take as much or as little time as they need to feel comfortable sharing. Connect with resources that are accessible for anyone who has experienced childhood abuse, including support groups and therapists that specialize in treating trauma and abuse.

It is crucial to respect your loved one's boundaries and choices. Continue offering support, as your loved one decides what to do with their past. Educate yourself about the impact of childhood abuse. It is confusing and difficult to understand the long-term effects of this type of trauma. If you find that you cannot tolerate hearing your loved ones' experience without trying to rescue or fix it, seek help for yourself. Consider reaching out to organizations like RAINN, which offer online support groups, resources, and chat boards that offer an abundance of suggestions and education.[2]

LOVING WITHOUT ENABLING

How can you support your loved ones, who were abused as children, without enabling? The act of enabling means to help someone in a way that perpetuates the problem rather than support the other person in solving the problem. Examples of enabling behaviors include making excuses for someone else's choices, covering up for them, or ignoring the problem entirely to avoid conflict. On many occasions I have worked with clients whose partners or loved ones enabled their destructive tendencies. Examples include buying large amounts of sweets, even though their loved ones are struggling with binge-eating tendencies. Other examples that I have encountered are partners who do not address self-harm such as superficial cutting. I worked with one woman whose husband would tend to her self-inflicted injuries, but he did not communicate his concern or set any boundaries with this type of behavior.

Loving someone who is dealing with the long-term aftermath of childhood abuse is complicated. Relationships are hard enough to navigate when there is no prior trauma history. Some of you may not have learned about your loved ones' traumatic past until years into the relationship. Secondary survivors are friends, family, parents, or partners of those that have suffered any type of childhood abuse.

It is normal to experience numbness or feel like your world has been torn apart when you find out something horrible happened to your loved one. Once your loved ones have disclosed more about their traumas, you may feel angry at the perpetrator, especially if it is someone you know. You may have urges to hurt that person. You may also feel angry at your loved one for not telling someone sooner or not reporting the abusers to the police. You may want to blame your loved ones, as if they somehow played a part in the abuse. Feeling angry is normal when someone you love has been hurt. It is important for you to look at your feelings and to find alternative outlets to manage your anger.

Some of you may find yourself feeling some kind of stigma, as if being in a relationship with your loved ones makes you worth less. You may worry too much about what others will think if they find out about your loved one's childhood trauma history. Shame is also a normal response if you have received messages of rape culture or have been ill-informed about other types of childhood abuse. Moving into a place of compassion and empathy will reduce your feelings of shame, and it will help you support your loved one without dismissing or minimizing what happened to them.

Often underneath shame are intense feelings of sadness. It is gut-wrenching to be a witness to the deep hurt that has been inflicted on people we love. You may worry too much about saying the right thing or feel like you constantly need to ask things like "Are you okay?" It is important to differentiate between someone being hurt versus someone being broken. You may feel like your loved one's life has been ruined by what was done to them. You may worry that you will never have a "normal" relationship once your loved one has disclosed acts of horror done to them.

You may feel responsible for fixing it, like you should have been able to do something to stop the abuse. Rather than focusing on the past, loved ones need to stay grounded and figure out how to stay present on the path toward healing. If you are stuck in any of these emotional responses after learning about your loved one's traumatic past, you may find yourself enabling or trying to fix their past. Some examples of enabling follow:

- Avoiding conversations or trying to cover up or make excuses for the abuse. For example, saying things like "Your parents did the best they could" or "Why can't you move on and stop thinking about your past?"

- Constantly coming to their rescue when they are acting on feelings of shame or rage.
- Putting your needs aside, even when your needs are a priority.

I worked with one client, whom I will refer to as Tom, who struggled with enabling tendencies for years in his marriage. His wife was sexually abused by her mother and emotionally neglected by her father. When Tom met his wife, he had no idea about her past. He started therapy with me because he was overwhelmed with her need to be taken care of. Tom told me that after his wife disclosed her abuse to him, she stopped being intimate. He told me that she became more demanding and angrier when she was diagnosed with breast cancer.

Once Tom learned about his wife's past, he told me he would do anything to stop her from feeling pain. He became isolated in his marriage, and he disconnected from his friends. After his wife began chemotherapy, Tom told me his life revolved around her treatment. He canceled his own medical appointments and social commitments if his wife was having flashbacks or nightmares. When Tom began therapy, he did not realize that he was enabling his wife to stay stuck in old patterns when she was triggered. Tom did not understand how his wife's cancer was stirring up times in her life when she felt exposed, violated, or vulnerable. He wanted to make life easier for her. He wanted to take away her pain from her past. Tom felt like it was his responsibility to eliminate his wife's triggers instead of encouraging her to seek therapy to address these underlying issues.

Like most of my clients, Tom was not just enabling his wife's patterns that re-created older traumas. Tom also had a history of emotional abuse and neglect in his childhood. We worked together for over two years before I was aware that Tom grew up in a family where he felt unheard and stranded. As his wife's codependency became more of a problem, he started getting in touch with some of his rage about times in his childhood when he felt dismissed. Tom was bullied by his peers, and he struggled with his academics. One day he walked into my office, and he said, "I have had enough of this. I am so sick of trying to fix my wife's problems and being made to feel like a bad husband when I try to set a limit." For weeks to follow, Tom and I discussed his pent-up anger and how he was trying to make everything better for his wife, because that is what he wanted from his parents when he was growing up. Eventually, Tom and I were able to identify that his enabling patterns came from the unconscious defense mechanism, projection. When people project, they feel their negative emotions or beliefs in someone else. Oftentimes, people project to protect themselves from internal conflict or anxiety.

As Tom spent more time talking in therapy about his reactions to his wife's abandonment issues, he was able to gain awareness about the part he played in his enabling patterns. Baggage from Tom's past was buried below his consciousness. When he witnessed his wife's despair and rage about her childhood, he saw his pain through her feelings. These emotions caused him anxiety, and instead of facing these feelings, he projected them onto his wife. He tried to be the person that protected her from any type of pain or anguish. Throughout our work together, Tom was able to identify what feelings he was avoiding as he enabled his wife to stay stuck in repetitive self-destructive patterns.

When Tom felt himself projecting, he gave himself permission to step away from the conversation so he could address feelings that were being activated. He was able to look at the situation with some more distance and could then make a different choice about how he responded to his wife. When he felt a rush of anxiety run throughout his body, he was able to slow down and talk back to that younger part of him that felt scared and responsible.

Actionable Steps You Can Take to Provide Emotional Support without Enabling

- Acknowledge that your loved one's situation is scary and that it is brave of them to find ways to regain control when their emotions feel out of control.
- Remember that you cannot rescue your loved ones from making decisions about their lives.
- Help them create a safety plan. For example, if your loved one resorts to self-destructive behaviors when they are triggered, write down five other choices they can make instead of using self-harm.
- Offer to go with your loved one to support groups or their individual therapy sessions, so you can be a witness and learn more about their experience.
- Help them identify a support network to assist with any of their physical needs.
- Encourage your loved one to participate in activities outside of their relationships with family or friends.
- Sit with your loved ones when they document memories or instances of abuse. Be a witness. Tell them you believe them and that it was not their fault.
- If your loved one is seeking legal repercussions, help them learn about the laws and find appropriate legal counsel.
- Find books or resources specifically written for loved ones of adult survivors of childhood abuse.

SUPPORT FOR PARTNERS AND FRIENDS OF SURVIVORS

In order to support your partners or friends who are survivors, it is important to understand the profound, long-lasting impact of childhood abuse. There are specific issues that survivors struggle with. Here are some of the most reported issues that survivors grapple with in their daily living.

- **Dissociation**: This is an unconscious defense that many survivors used as children to stay sane and detach from the emotional, physical, or sexual harm inflicted on them. While their bodies are physically present, their minds go to a completely different place. Imagine driving to your friend's house and thinking, I have no idea how I got here. Another example of dissociation is when a survivor talks about their memories, but they act as if it happened to someone else. Think about when your loved ones disclosed their abuse. They may talk about it with no emotion, and you may notice that they struggle to look at you or express any feeling about what they are sharing. It can be upsetting to witness your loved one looking out of touch with reality. Try and stay calm. It helps if you can be a safe presence, even if your loved one is upset or scared.

- **Triggers**: Survivors might jump or have a startle response when you get too close. Have you ever noticed your loved one flinching when you approach them with any type of physical contact? Certain words, smells, actions, or gestures can send your loved ones into a heightened state of alert. If your loved ones understand their triggers, you can help them avoid them or be more prepared when the dissociative symptoms get activated. You may want to offer support by suggesting grounding activities. You can talk with your loved one about what helps them to feel more grounded. Do they feel safe when they sit in their garden, or go for a walk, or even walk barefoot on the sand at a beach? If your loved one has developed a list of grounding techniques, this would be the appropriate time to remind them that they have choices about how to react in that moment.

- **Self-Harm**: If your loved one is hurting themself or struggling with active suicidal ideation, it can feel overwhelming and scary. You may panic or want to take your loved one to the emergency room. The way you respond to your loved one will have an impact on how much they open up to you about their self-harming tendencies. Keep in mind that self-harm is usually someone's way of managing very hard feelings or experiences. There are several ways you can help when your partner discloses these types of behaviors. Try not to judge the behavior. Let your loved one know you are there for them. Try and relate to their feelings rather than focus on the self-harming behaviors. With their help, remove all objects that are sharp or can be used to cut off circulation, such as scarves. Talk to your loved one about the qualities you love most about them.

- **Suicidal Ideation**: Different people have different ways of feeling suicidal. Some people feel this way because they feel hopeless and inundated with horrific memories and feelings from their childhood. Others describe feeling unbearable pain that others cannot imagine. It is important to understand that suicide comes from feeling trapped or as if they have no other choice. Usually, survivors go to the darkest of places emotionally when they are fighting their truth. For some survivors, suicidality is part of their memories. There were many times during my adolescence that I wanted to be gone. I felt trapped, hopeless, and unprotected. Through therapy, I learned that when I was feeling suicidal as an adult, it was partly memory. My therapist used to ask me, "Does that feeling match the present?" She would also remind me that I already survived and that I had my whole life ahead of me. If your loved one is expressing the wish to die, do not take that personally. It is not you that they want to escape from. It is the pain and shame from the past that often leads to despair. This is a good time to remind your loved one of all they have to look forward to. You can suggest that your loved one write down all their accomplishments or goals for the future.

Whenever I wanted to end my life, I pulled out a list of hopes and wishes for my future. I told myself repeatedly, "I am here on earth with a purpose. I am going to be a voice of change for survivors, and I want to be a mom and have a family." I shared that wish with some of my close friends and colleagues. If I did not feel strong enough to hold onto hope, my friends and colleagues would remind me of that statement. They left me voicemails and sent me emails. If you feel like your loved one is not able to take in the love you are offering at the moment, write them a note, leave them a voicemail, or put sticky notes in their bags with statements of love and hope. Keep in mind that even if your loved ones are closed off in the moment, they still can hear what you are telling them.

- **Making Healthy Choices**: Another issue to think about is that your loved one may struggle with making healthy choices. They may be feeling worthless or have low self-esteem. They may be finding themselves in intimate connections with people who do not respect them or put themselves in unsafe situations. I worked in therapy with one father whose daughter put herself in a string of unhealthy relationships after she was assaulted as a young teen. Before she started therapy, she was spending time with men that were much older than her, many of whom also assaulted her. Her father was devastated, and he could not understand why his daughter would be attracted to such "lowlifes," as he referred to them. Over time he realized that his daughter was re-creating and reenacting the assault that happened to her as a young teen. While she had told her father that she was raped, she was unwilling to go to therapy or get help. She told her father, "I just want to forget about it." We helped him develop strategies to manage his rage and disappointment about the choices she was making, and eventually he was able to help his daughter get into treatment to address the assault.

- **Physical or Emotional Intimacy**: Most survivors avoid any situation where there is physical or emotional intimacy. This can be incredibly frustrating for loved ones, and it is hard not to personalize their unwillingness to be vulnerable. I was in therapy with one survivor who refused to have any physical contact with her husband after she started having memories of ritual abuse. A few months after we started focusing on her trauma history, she came to session announcing she was never going to let her husband touch her "ever again." She flinched at the slightest gesture of physical intimacy. Once she felt comfortable in our relationship, she invited her husband in for a session. We talked with her husband about the process of uncovering childhood abuse, and I gave him some resources to help him understand what was going on in my client's body and heart. As the months went on, my client talked more to her husband about what happened to her and how she wanted to move through this part of her dreadful past. About a year into therapy, she decided to go inpatient because she wanted to immerse herself in her recovery and reclaim her right to feel safe with the man she chose to marry. When she went into residential treatment, her husband joined her in therapy sessions, and they talked about ways to reconnect physically. If you are feeling hopeless about the possibility of having intimacy with your partners, make space for hope. As survivors work through the dissociation, triggers, and shame, they are much more likely to connect on a deeper level.

- **Shame**: The most challenging part for many survivors is working through the shame they have been carrying during and after the abuse occurred. Many survivors feel broken. It takes a lot of patience and stamina to stand by your loved one as they muddle through shame. Offering support to someone who is experiencing shame does not mean you need to fix it or distract your loved one from the feeling. A great place to start is to join your loved one by offering empathy and letting your loved one know you have felt shame, even if it was unrelated to childhood trauma. Saying things like "I'm with you no matter what" or "I know you feel like you have been broken, but you are not! You have been hurt, and I can support you in your emotional wounds and healing."

Recently, I started seeing someone in therapy who was experiencing what she called "PTSD backslides." I started working with my client—I will refer to as Melissa—about three years ago. When I met her, she was married with two small children. She had been to therapy in her late teens, after surviving emotional and physical abuse as a child. Melissa went off to college and she got her degree in teaching. She met who she thought was a wonderful man when she was in her early twenties. Melissa dated Shaun for about two years, and then they got married. Melissa told me that she started seeing red flags very early in their relationship, but she did not let herself know the truth. She told me that the behaviors he exhibited were like those she saw in her childhood.

Months after Melissa gave birth to her second child, she decided she'd had enough. She said that Shaun "belittled me for everything from how I dressed to how I parented." She said that Shaun was violent when he drank alcohol and that he ruined two cars and sent them into a financial crisis because he lost one job after another. One night after Shaun came home drunk, Melissa told me that she grabbed a few things and both of her children, and she went to stay with her parents. She spent the next several months gathering her thoughts and handling legal business because she wanted a divorce. She started therapy with me because she wanted to understand what drew her to an abusive narcissist. Melissa wanted a partner that she could feel safe with.

About six months after I met Melissa, she walked into my office for a session and she announced with a huge smile, "I met someone, and he is totally different from Shaun." For the next few months Melissa continued to date her new boyfriend, David, as she worked through childhood abuse and the divorce from Shaun. Once Melissa felt more comfortable with David, she began taking more risks in that relationship. Like most survivors, Melissa was hit with strong emotions each time she experienced the contrast between a healthy relationship and an abusive relationship. There was a period of a few months in our sessions when Melissa talked about having what she called "PTSD backslides." She described feeling panic, a loss of control in her body, and a feeling of doom and gloom. Melissa knew that the emotions she was having with David were not about their connection. We talked at length about how David could support Melissa through these painful moments. David did not have a childhood abuse history. At first Melissa was worried that he would not be able to support her because he could not understand PTSD and what it felt like to be triggered.

I asked Melissa what she needed from David when she felt detached or disconnected. She said she wanted a witness. She wanted David to acknowledge what she was feeling, even if he could not understand what it was like to be in her body and mind. Melissa was terrified that David would leave her if she continued to have "PTSD backslides." She was brave and was able to voice her concerns to David. She told him that she needed him to check in and reassure her that he was there with her.

Melissa wrote out a list of questions or statements he could say when she was struggling. She told David she wanted to rewire her brain and build trust and supportive neural relationship pathways to replace the old ones from her childhood and from her marriage with Shaun. Melissa's ability to communicate her needs and educate David helped both of them establish healthy boundaries. These boundaries and suggestions on how to support her in difficult moments enabled them to move ahead in their relationship. Melissa reiterated that she did not need David to fix her or try to make her feel better. She wanted David to sit with her or be with her when old feelings of shame, rage, or fear crept between their connection. She encouraged David to find support for himself so that if he felt overwhelmed or at a loss of what to do, he also had people to talk to.

Actionable Healing Statements Loved Ones and Friends Can Use with Childhood Abuse Survivors

- I believe you.
- I admire your courage and strength.
- I cannot imagine what that was like for you.
- It was not your fault!
- You are not alone. I care about you, and I am here to listen or help in any way that you need.
- This should not have happened to you.
- You are a warrior.
- You can do this!
- Think about all the people that love you.
- Stay in the fight; it is worth it.
- I am honored that you would share this with me.
- This must be so painful for you.
- You made it. You can do this part.
- I do not judge you.
- You are not broken; you were hurt and now you are healing.

Actionable Healing Steps Loved Ones and Friends Can Take to Support Survivors

- Always ask before making gestures of physical contact.
- Offer to give space if your loved one is inconsolable.
- Have a safety plan or keep a list of phone numbers and resources.
- Accept silence. Be present and calm in moments of turbulence or turmoil.
- Do not speak badly of your loved one's perpetrator or abuser.
- Write notes or leave messages filled with words of love and encouragement.
- Reach out to your loved ones on holidays, birthdays, or anniversaries.
- Allow your loved one to say whatever they want about the people that abused them.
- Offer to help with childcare, encourage them to take a mental health day, help with daily chores, plan a day out of the house in nature or an environment that is quiet and nurturing.

CHAPTER 9

Rebuilding Trust in Yourself and Others

INTEGRATING CHILDHOOD MEMORIES INTO ADULTHOOD

The goal in healing is to integrate the cut-off feelings of abuse into part of our daily existence, into our lives today. Then we can recognize what is about *then* and what is about *now*. Memories of abuse are unbearable at times, overwhelming and unbelievable. In order to survive, we needed to distance ourselves and turn off our reactions as abuse occurred. Once we break our silence and process our earlier childhood traumas, we need to regain consciousness of our buried feelings and tend to the parts of our younger selves that felt scared, ashamed, and betrayed.

Talking about what happened to us does not undo the trauma, but if we deal with our memories and feelings, we can understand the impact. We can deal with the sensations we experience in our bodies when we are triggered. We can learn to let go of that constant sense of danger and self-hate. Integrating childhood memories into adulthood is about learning how to face life's trials and tribulations without becoming enraged, ashamed, or defeated. The first step in the integration process is using the coping mechanisms we have developed when we are flooded with body memories and emotional memories from the past.

Many of my clients who have a history of physical, sexual, and emotional abuse struggle with staying in their bodies when old feelings are activated. For years during my healing, I lived in a body that felt different sensations from my abuse whenever I felt stranded, unsafe, or distrusting of myself and others. Repeatedly, my therapist would ask me what I was trying to tell myself when I did not feel safe in my body. The first several times Dorothy asked me this, I felt like my head was going to explode. I was enraged with Dorothy for asking me such a question. I felt like she was telling me that I was making up what I was feeling. Then I would think that she did not believe any of what I told her.

Over time, I started to notice a pattern. When I questioned my truth or when I shamed myself for being an incest survivor, my body would feel like it was being violated all over again. I felt many graphic aspects of the sexual harm inflicted onto me by my father. There were days when I lived life as if I was on automatic pilot. The only emotions I felt were self-hate, disgust, despair, and rage. These feelings went with me into my therapy sessions and into all of my close friendships. I felt undeserving of feeling love or support, and I would start to disconnect from all of my relationships. When I sat with Dorothy in therapy, she would tell me she felt like I was pushing her away. Repeatedly, Dorothy would tell me that she felt like I was not hearing her or taking in what she was saying. She would ask me if I noticed that I was describing my friends or coworkers as if they were perpetrators. My unresolved trauma about being abused by my father consumed me. When my body felt like it was being assaulted, I was preoccupied with those memories. I went into protective mode so I would not get hurt again.

Part of integrating childhood memories into adulthood means we need to find other ways to manage horror, dissociation, and disconnection. When I was flooded with body memories and flashbacks, it felt like I was trying to scream back at my unconscious. I wanted so much to believe that I was crazy and that I was making up all the memories of abuse. One of the hardest things to accept about childhood trauma is that we will never be able to remember in detail all our memories, whether we repressed or suppressed our traumas. We will never be able to know every detail in consequential order. My body was telling me, "You were abused. You are not making it up. You need to find a way to accept the truth." The remarkable thing about our minds is that it allows our body to store the memories and hold them in our unconscious until we are in a place in our lives as adults when we can tolerate and work through our past. A significant part of the healing process is to be able to understand and tolerate the sensations, memories, and feelings that intrude on our functioning in the present. Moving out of the fight-or-flight responses requires us to have awareness when that phenomenon is occurring. It means pulling together the part of our brains that split off and dissociated.

I worked with one client whom I will refer to as Maddy. I started seeing Maddy as a teenager. She developed an eating disorder during her freshman year of high school. She had a tenuous relationship with her mother and her father was out of the picture most of her childhood. Maddy did not start talking about the sexual abuse by her sister until she graduated college and was financially independent. She left therapy in her senior year of high school and then returned after she graduated from college.

She did not start dissociating in our sessions until she came back to therapy. Maddy came back to therapy because she was in a physically and sexually abusive relationship with a man. After a few months of talking in our sessions about her boyfriend, she decided to bring him in for a session. Maddy told me she wanted me to observe her reactions to him when they sat in a room together. I was shocked at the difference in Maddy's effect when her boyfriend sat in my office with her. She became timid, lost eye contact, and shut down. At one point in that session her boyfriend turned red in the face as he yelled at her about something trivial. I felt like I was sitting in the room with a much younger and scared Maddy.

Moments after they left the appointment, Maddy texted me. She asked me if it seemed like she felt unsafe with him. While I could not feel what was going on in her body, I noticed that I became slightly dissociated toward the end of that session. When Maddy came in for her next session, we talked about what she felt and what I noticed. We were able to help Maddy understand that her reaction to her boyfriend stemmed from earlier abuse done to her by her older sister.

Maddy was heartbroken that she found herself in an intimate relationship with an abuser. However, she was also able to understand that she was drawn to her boyfriend because he felt familiar. She was used to being controlled, humiliated, and taken advantage of. No one ever talked to Maddy about dissociation or that her eating disorder developed partly because she was unable to stay in her body when she was triggered.

Maddy worked hard in therapy for the next couple of years, integrating her childhood and developing coping strategies when she began to dissociate. Maddy made a timeline, including a list of warning signs with old boyfriends. She noticed that she allowed herself to stay in situations where her safety was at risk because she did not understand dissociation and how that was unconsciously trying to help her stay present. We talked about times when her gut instincts were telling her to leave and how she would act against these feelings. Maddy also began to understand that the past came alive in her body when she was with men who treated her poorly.

About two years after Maddy broke up with her boyfriend, she met another man and began dating him. For the first few months of their relationship, Maddy noticed that she began to leave her body when he showed the slightest amount of disapproval. One day she came to session, and she told me, "I am so sick of feeling unsafe, and I want to be able to stay in my body so

I can figure out if the person I am with in the present is safe." It was a pivotal moment in our work together because she was making a conscious choice to break an unconscious defense. Maddy developed the awareness that if she could not tap into her gut feelings, she would not be able to distinguish between safety and danger in the present.

About six months into her newest relationship, Maddy opened up about an incident when she went into fight or flight and left her body. She had just gotten out of the shower, and she said her boyfriend at the time entered the bathroom. Before he even began to speak, Maddy told me she could feel her body tingling and her heart racing. She told me, "The second he walked into the bathroom I panicked." As we continued the conversation, Maddy began dissociating in our session. Tears were pouring down her cheeks, and she expressed feeling like her heart had just broken. I asked her if the feelings she was having matched the moment. Maddy told me that she left the bathroom door open and that her boyfriend came in to grab a towel. She said from the moment he started saying something about trying not to get water on the floor, she felt unsafe. She said there were seconds when all she could see was her boyfriend's mouth moving but that she could not hear any actual words coming out of his mouth.

As Maddy and I processed this PTSD moment, she leaned forward in her chair, and she told me, "I am so sick of feeling like I am being threatened or assaulted when my boyfriend looks remotely irritated or annoyed. I stopped Maddy and affirmed the importance of what she was saying. I heard Maddy telling me that she was aware that her mind and body were slipping into freeze mode because she was triggered. For years, Maddy was unable to identify when this was happening. In the past, Maddy would shut down and disconnect from people when she was triggered. We talked about how this experience was different. The part of her that felt frustrated at her reaction was healthy and hopeful. In order to integrate her history of abuse done to her by her sister, she needed to allow herself to understand her triggers and identify what is about the past rather than what is happening in the present.

Christine Courtois, a renowned trauma and abuse expert, developed a sequence of events that clients can use as they work toward integration.[1] Like Maddy and dozens of other clients I have worked with, the first step is to work toward safety and stabilization. The next part of healing is about processing the trauma, as Maddy had done in therapy when she returned for the second time. The last step is focused on integration, as described in Maddy's story. Dr. Courtois developed treatment goals for complex PTSD.[2] They are as follows:

- restore self-esteem,
- restore psychosocial reactions,
- develop trust in others,
- develop connections with others,
- restore the physical and spiritual self, and
- decrease episodes of revictimization and reenactments of abuse.

As we process and resolve earlier events of trauma, we can focus on life choices and how to manage our feelings as we rebuild trust in ourselves and others. This part of treatment can last for years. Our memories of the abuse never completely dissipate. Most of us will experience triggers, like Maddy, which are reminders of our past. As we saw Maddy and her reaction when her boyfriend entered the bathroom, our bodies always remembered the memories we hid in our brains. You may be asking, why does this happen?

Memories surface when they do because a part of us knows we are safe and that we are capable of knowing the truth, no matter how painful. There is always going to be a younger part of ourselves that is inside and holding onto our childhood memories. As we become adults and have more time away from the abuse, these memories come back because there is a part of us that wants to be heard and understood. There is a part of us that wants to heal and knows that we cannot integrate our childhood until we allow ourselves to know what happened and understand the impact. When anger, sadness, confusion, heartache, hypervigilance, and panic come out, we need to find a way to sit with these feelings and find a way to place them. Making space to be in the present requires us to revisit these emotions and utilize the coping skills to navigate in our relationships today.

Earlier in the book I spoke about the process of remembering and managing PTSD and flashbacks. We could not have dealt with these memories or emotions as the traumas occurred because that would have been too painful and felt unsafe. Part of integrating is about building relationships with people in the present that can serve as a witness or supporter. It can take time to figure out who are the best people to lean on and be vulnerable with. It can take years in therapy to learn how to decipher the difference between abusive versus safe and appropriate responses with others.

Actionable Steps to Integrating Childhood Memories into Adulthood

- Differentiate being triggered and being threatened.
- Reassure yourself that you are not going crazy. You are not sliding backward; you are digging deeper.
- Focus on your job or something that is meaningful as you confront another aspect of your past. This will allow you to have some distance from the pain and horror and fear that are triggered from the memories.
- When you are having body memories or slipping into freeze mode, remind yourself that your body is remembering how you held the fear during the abuse. Take a

moment and remind yourself that body memories are part of the flashback. Talk back to your body. You can say things like "I am safe now," or ask yourself, "What is my body trying to tell me?"

- Acknowledge the years when you didn't feel safe or when you were in danger.

- Talk about the younger parts of yourself that went into a state of panic, and try and use your adult voice to comfort those younger parts.

- Allow yourself to describe these younger parts and their feelings at the time. As you talk about these parts, you are making space to contain these emotions and leave them in the past.

- Step into your intellect and use that part of your mind to address these traumatic responses from your childhood. You can say things like "Gosh, you must have been terrified" or "Your mind and body did such a great job protecting you from such horror."

- Imagine being an adult as your childhood parts surface. What would that adult say to your hurt younger self?

- Work on forgiveness. That does not mean forgetting what happened or letting your abusers off the hook. It is about accepting any negative feelings you are having and validating that those feelings are appropriate because of what happened to you. Forgiveness is a choice. You can forgive and not forget. You can forgive and keep your abusers or perpetrators out of your lives.

- Practice gratitude. Focus on your bravery and your willingness to face your truth. It takes a tremendous amount of courage to move into the integration process and allow yourself to develop a safe and fulfilling adulthood.

- Feel gratitude for the environment you are creating, and give yourself credit for taking this important step.
- Continue to practice self-care. When you go through periods of time when you are having more flashbacks or symptoms of PTSD, do not shame yourself or get discouraged. Instead, be curious and think about how this is another opportunity that will lead to more happiness and tranquility moving forward.
- Continue spending time with your supporters, friends, and family by choice. Keep going to therapy. Keep reaching out.
- The only way out of pain from our past is to move through it, with compassion, kindness, and determination.

Inner Child Healing and Keeping Old Feelings in the Past

To heal from our traumatic past, we need to attend to all the parts of our fragmented selves and find a way to nurture and acknowledge all our feelings. In other words, as we integrate the parts of ourselves that were hurt, we need to flip the self-hate and disconnection into self-compassion. Recently, there has been much more attention in the media on inner child healing. Tanya Fruehauf, a therapist based in Vancouver, talks about the importance of reparenting our inner child.[3] How does inner child work help us keep old feelings in the past?

As we work through our childhoods and gain awareness about all that was lost in childhood, we can attend to and heal these parts of ourselves. Integrating memories of abuse does not heal us unless we develop the tools to be able to better protect ourselves and understand how to respond to our triggers without going into shame.

Inner child healing doesn't happen overnight. It took me years to accept that this was and continues to be an integral part of my healing. Most of my clients look at me like I have ten heads when

I try to explain what inner child healing means. Throughout the years I have learned that tending to my younger self promotes a feeling of autonomy and confidence. It also helps to contain the shame by refusing to continue using self-destructive behaviors to mask feelings that we want to avoid.

One of the most important parts of my healing focused on the pregnancies and miscarriages I had because of the abuse done to me by my father. I was pregnant for the first time when I was fourteen years old. It took me several years to put this part of my past together and find a way to live with this truth. After five years in intensive trauma work, I broke my silence about a miscarriage I had during my freshman year of high school.

One day in late July, I went for a run around the neighborhood. I was feeling self-conscious about weight gain, and I was trying to take control of my body, which felt completely out of control. For weeks I was counting the number of days I was late for my next menstrual cycle. It had been one hundred days since my last period. I remembered thinking, "Get it out of me," as the cramping started. I was running down the sidewalk and was overtaken by intense pain. I made myself continue to run, but only made it another half a block. I collapsed on the sidewalk and just lay there thinking, "Someone help me!" At that time, I was dissociated and confused and thinking I finally got my period! I was relieved, but I was also horrified. On some level I knew I was having a miscarriage.

About ten minutes after I fell to the ground, I heard an ambulance siren. The first thing I thought when I realized they were coming for me was that I hope they do not call my parents. I begged the EMT workers not to tell anyone. I was fourteen years old. Back then these types of statements did not set off alarms in the healthcare profession.

When I arrived at the hospital, I saw my mother coming down the hallway. Doctors told my mother that I needed to have a pregnancy test. The doctor repeatedly asked me, "Is there any chance you could be pregnant?" I responded vehemently, "I am a virgin." My mother told the doctors not to give me a pregnancy test. When the doctors took me back into the exam room, my body extricated the fetus. I felt immense pain. I focused on the blue paint on the walls, and I remember feeling like I was in a bad dream.

The doctors told me and my mother that I had passed a clot. They explained that without a pregnancy test they could not give a clear determination of what happened. This memory came back in bits and pieces. Throughout the months when I told Dorothy about this trauma, I felt despair and shame. I called myself disparaging names, and I spent hours locked in my bedroom after those therapy sessions. I could not tolerate the magnitude of this experience or feel any type of relief about speaking. I kept saying to Dorothy, "How could my mom do this? I know she knew I was pregnant." I blamed myself for having miscarriages. I hated myself and I could not accept that my own father would get me pregnant. Healing this part of my past is something I will continue to do for the rest of my life.

Anything can trigger these memories, whether it is being late for my period as I enter menopause or when I was pregnant with my little man twelve years ago. It is a process to heal this part of my inner child. Once I was able to come to terms with the truth, I could begin to give my younger self compassion and love. Instead of hating myself and my body I have learned to love and tend to these younger parts. When I was pregnant with my little man, I went into a deep depression at the end of my first trimester. There were a lot of reminders of what I noticed when I was pregnant as a teen. I remembered the feeling of my swollen belly. I remembered watching my weight go up. I remembered the tenderness of my breasts.

When I saw the picture of the ultrasound at the end of my first trimester, I felt like I was looking at images of multiple fetuses that were in my body as a teenager. The turning point came when I entered my second trimester. For the first time on my journey, I could grieve and cry for my younger self. It was like a switch went off in my brain, and I found a way to come to terms with this part of my past. I could talk in therapy about miscarriages without hating myself. I developed coping strategies to stay in the present when I had these types of flashbacks. I focused on the miracle of conceiving after trying to get pregnant for almost one year. I did things like sit in a bathtub and love my pregnant belly. I wrote messages of hope on pieces of paper that I hung on my bedroom mirror. I reached out to a few close friends and asked them to leave me voicemails, reminding me that I was worthy of having a healthy pregnancy at age forty.

Even today, as I write this part of my book, I am flooded with flashbacks. As these memories emerge, I am talking to my younger self and finding ways to comfort the teenage Shari Botwin, who felt scared, horrified, and betrayed. I have reached out to some friends who knew me when I was working through this part of my past. I am wrapping my arms around my heart and body and reminding myself, "You are okay. You made it through and look at the life you have created." I am watching my younger self that fell apart in therapy as I spoke about this part of my past. I am actively focused on staying present and using multiple self-care strategies to manage the feelings.

Childhood abuse shapes the way we live, the way we feel about ourselves, and the way we make sense of the world we lived in growing up. Children flourish when they have adults who protect them and can tune into their distress. Earlier trauma causes adult survivors to spend most of their energy fighting off danger, which does not allow them to give and receive care, love, and nurturing.

The path toward healing and reclaiming our adulthoods is understanding how to heal our younger selves. In order to do that, we need to stop protecting our parents or the people that caused us harm. Instead, we need to learn how to reparent our inner child, which means making sure we feel the love and safety we lacked in childhood. We need to develop tools to better protect ourselves and understand our triggers. We need to learn how to depend on others and trust that there are people in this world that can love us in healthy ways. We need to stop feeling like we need to keep ourselves alone in order to be safe. We need to form a tribe of supportive friends and loved ones that give us a sense of safety and community.

In order to be in the moment, we need to know where we are and what is going on around us. If our body is not in sync with our brains, we need to place the feelings coming up that are not about today. One of the most important steps on our healing journey is learning how to stop old wounds from destroying our relationships in the present. In most instances, old feelings creep in as we are connecting with partners, friends, therapists, supervisors, and role models.

How do we let go of our defenses and risk being hurt? We deserve relationships and many of us will struggle to stay in these connections. Every time we make contact with someone or begin to let ourselves form a relationship, we are at risk of being triggered. Many of us have built up layers of armor to stop others from hurting us again. The problem is that as adults, we no longer need these devices to keep ourselves safe and aware of our surroundings. Unresolved trauma or heartbreak about being hurt by a trusted adult can consume us, even years after we break our silence.

How can we recognize when old feelings are wreaking havoc and getting in the way of current relationships? One thing to pay attention to is how often you are fighting with your significant other, your therapist, or even a close friend. The presence of old feelings may not be in our awareness. Part of the integration process is about gaining awareness when unconscious beliefs or patterns play out in the present.

There are a few questions you can ask yourself to decipher what is about the *past* and what is about *today*. Are the fights you are having repetitive, or do they have similar themes? Is your reaction to something within the relationship more intense than what matches the moment. Do you find that you have a difficult time shifting once you are triggered?

If you are unable to decipher where your feelings are coming from in the moment, consider asking yourself questions like "When did the conversation get hard?" or "Am I shutting down?" or "Do I need a minute?" If you try and slow down the conversation, you are giving yourself a chance to process what just happened. It is okay to ask yourself, "Where is this feeling coming from?" or "Does this response feel familiar?" If you feel yourself getting heated up or flighty, take a minute to regroup. Go back to your grounding strategies and remember that feelings come and go. We do not need to disengage when old feelings are showing up in our relationships. We may just need to give ourselves space. We may need to evaluate our emotions and figure out if they match the moment.

Our pain from the past does not need to continue to harm us. Our childhood wounds are proof of our resilience, strength, and courage, and now we can use them to have healthier relationships as adults. If we allow ourselves to flee once we are activated, we are not allowing ourselves to heal and have a different experience in the present. When we have a strong reaction to a partner, friend, supervisor, or therapist, we can sit with this feeling and ask ourselves, "What does this remind me of?" Some of the answers we may have include "This reminds me of when my mother belittled me, or when my father abused me." Some of us may remember feeling these emotions even in our early childhood.

Through the years I have had a repetitive thought of feeling like a total misfit. I remember being a young child and thinking that I was different from all the other kids. I never felt like I fit in. I thought people hated me and that no one wanted to be around me. Even in my fifties, I experience this emotion. Recently, I was hanging out with a bunch of soccer moms while my kiddo was playing soccer. I listened to the other mothers talk about their lives, and I felt like I did not belong and that I was not wanted in that group. I have felt this way for decades. Anytime I am with others whoI assume had "normal" childhoods, I feel like I want to disappear.

I decided to share these thoughts with two of the other soccer moms. Here is how that conversation went:

> I felt like a total misfit at soccer today. Like I don't fit in, and people don't like me. The truth is I don't like some people, ha-ha, and it is probably all projections and insecurities. Allison wrote back, "Glad you know it is a projection. You fit in just perfectly. And we all love you for who you are. We all feel like we don't fit in sometimes." I answered, "Yep, I remember you saying that to me before. Being single with a group of so many feels so weird. No one wants to ask about someone who was abused by their own father. It's just the way it is. It's too hard to understand and most people want to act like it didn't happen." Allison responded, "I totally get it." Later that night Laurie chimed in saying, "I am just catching up, I am sorry. Shari, we all love you and if there is anything we can do to make you feel more included please let us know. People love you because of who you are, it doesn't matter what happened to you in the past. We support you one hundred percent. I didn't know you felt that way?" Then Allison wrote, "We love you and see you for the awesome person you are." Laurie answered, "I second that!"

Actionable Steps to Healing Our Inner Child

- Make a gratitude journal. Go out and buy a notebook. Plaster it with pictures of quotes that affirm your strength and bravery during your childhood. If you feel like it will help, also include photos of your younger self. Some prompts you can write about are things you are grateful for today, such as what you have learned in the past that helps you live a better life today, adults that supported you during the abuse, and some obstacles you were able to overcome today.

- Create a section in your journal that focuses on your self-esteem. Write about at least five things that made you feel admired and affirmed. Write about the highlight of your week when you were able to accomplish a goal or set a boundary.

- Create a section in your journal that focuses on self-love. You can write about what you admire about yourself and your ability to survive. If you are struggling with feelings of regret or guilt, write about how you can forgive yourself. Write about three qualities that others complimented you on this week.

- Find ways to hug yourself every day. Practice the butterfly hug. Cross your hands over your chest and link your thumbs together. Tap your chest with your left hand and then right hand. Observe your thoughts and feelings and imagine people who love you wrapping their arms around you.

- Think about a moment in your childhood that made you happy. Maybe it was spending time with a grandparent or performing dance or going to a park. Give yourself a few minutes each day to connect with your inner child and times that helped you to survive. If you cannot remember a happy childhood moment, think about a person from your childhood grabbing hold of your hand and taking you to that happy place.

- Take a look in the mirror and reframe negative thoughts. For example, instead of telling yourself you don't matter or that no one loves you, say "I do matter," and "I am loveable," and "My voice matters."

- Use self-compassion instead of self-judgment.
- Make time to play each day. Skip, sing, dance, and laugh. Picture your younger self being able to play without being weighed down by memories of trauma. Give yourself permission to laugh at yourself. It is never too late to connect to that inner child who wanted to be free and not have a care in the world. Grab a coloring book, play with clay or LEGO bricks, run barefoot on the beach, or watch your favorite cartoon.

Signs that you are healing your inner child:

1. You are replacing self-destructive behaviors with healthy coping mechanisms.

2. You are facing challenges rather than avoiding them.

3. You are quieting your inner critic.

4. You can identify your needs and set limits.

5. You can regulate your emotions when you are triggered.

6. You give yourself permission to play and be silly.

7. You are more structured and able to accomplish daily rituals.

CHAPTER 10

Flipping Horror into Hope

PARENTING AFTER CHILDHOOD ABUSE

One of the most devastating effects of surviving childhood abuse is it often leaves people feeling inadequate and fearful about starting their own families. Think about your perception of adults when you were a child. Think about how many times you told yourselves that you would never want to be a parent as you were growing up. How many times have you thought that if you chose to start a family of your own after having been abused as a child that you would become an abusive parent?

While the statistics are alarming about intergenerational abuse, the truth is that many survivors of childhood abuse will go on to be loving, healthy parents. Chances are you would not have chosen to read this book if you really believed that you are incapable of breaking the cycle of abuse, even if it goes back generations in your biological family.

Being an abuse survivor does not mean that you are destined to be parents that harm your own children—physically, sexually, or emotionally. Throughout the book we have explored the hope that comes with knowing, understanding, and healing from our traumatic past. We have focused on different themes in the healing process and how to work through all kinds of feelings, including fear, shame, anger, and grief. We have focused on different healing strategies that will allow us to live our lives in adulthood feeling safe and supported.

Through the healing process we have given ourselves the opportunity to identify distinct roles we have played; in addition to being a survivor. As we move through this process of recovery, we give ourselves the chance to fulfill lifelong goals and dreams that we once felt were impossible.

For years I told Dorothy I would never get married or have children. The thought of being pregnant terrified me. My perception of parents was that they were distrusting and dangerous. I thought it was impossible to parent a child after living with parents who acted in abusive ways. When I started therapy with Dorothy, I was twenty-five years old. At that time, I was barely functioning. I could not fathom the idea of taking care of an innocent child. There were many days when I did not want to get out of bed, eat, get dressed, or go to work. I would think about children and imagine being neglectful and distant, because at that time I did not fully trust anyone.

As I went through the healing process and got a bit older, I noticed a shift in my feelings about having a family of my own. After therapy one day, I was sobbing on the phone with a friend, telling her I wished I had never opened my big mouth and that I did not want to be alive anymore. She suggested that I get a dog. My first reaction to her was "Are you crazy?" I never had a dog, and I had no idea what being a pet owner would be like.

The next week I decided to listen to my friend, and I got myself the best dog ever. I adopted a dog named Chloe, and for years she was a source of light and hope. At times I found myself struggling with what I call "mom guilt," and other triggers. For example, I had a tough time separating from Chloe, because I felt like I was abandoning her if I left her home for more than a couple of hours. I talked to Dorothy and some of my friends who had dogs. I thought about where that feeling was coming from, and often discovered that I was projecting my own feelings of abandonment onto Chloe. There were other times when I felt undeserving of having Chloe. I remember one time after I had spoken about a miscarriage I had during my abuse as a young teenager, telling Dorothy that I was going to find Chloe a new home. I was consumed with shame, and I felt like the miscarriage was my fault.

When feelings of inadequacy and worthlessness crept into my heart and body, I had to work hard not to act on these emotions. I loved Chloe and I realized that when I felt like a terrible daughter or an awful person, I felt undeserving of having something in my life that brought me joy and hope. As the years went by and I had Chloe longer, I started to get in touch with my yearning to be a mother. When I was in my early thirties, I started thinking more about having children. I could imagine coming home from work and taking care of an infant. I could imagine nurturing and loving a child. I could picture managing triggers of parenthood, because I had a therapist and some friends and colleagues who knew about my abuse.

When I was around thirty-five years old, I was diagnosed and treated for thyroid cancer. That experience changed my perception of myself and what I wanted for my life moving forward. Many people reminded me that this was "a good cancer to have," if you are going to have cancer. That is not how I reacted to the diagnosis.

Weeks after I had my first surgery to remove part of my thyroid, I thought more about my future and the relationship I had formed with Chloe. I knew I was not going to live forever, and I was sick of letting my history dictate my choices moving forward. Being a dog parent taught me a lot about myself, and it proved to me that I could take care of something besides myself.

A year after I was treated for cancer, I started thinking more seriously about having a child. I wanted to get married and parent with a partner, but I had broken up with my first serious boyfriend months after I was treated for thyroid cancer. I knew time was running out if I wanted to conceive and carry a pregnancy. At first, I considered going the adoption route, because having a pregnancy meant I would have to face memories of miscarriages in my adolescence. It felt impossible to make a choice that would force me to relive memories of unwanted pregnancies.

About three months after I started looking into adopting a child, I changed my mind. I had one of those light bulb moments in therapy. I told Dorothy I did not want to keep letting what happened to me stop me from living the life I wanted as an adult. The truth was I wanted to be pregnant. I wanted to experience the miracle of life and reclaim my body's ability to conceive.

I spent over a year working with an infertility doctor, trying to get pregnant. During that time, I worked on letting go of some of my fears and unresolved shame. Each time I had a failed pregnancy attempt, part of me thought that was happening because I did not deserve to be a parent. I talked at length with Dorothy and some close friends about bringing a child into this world without a partner or parents. I was determined to move forward and disarm, feeling unworthy of starting a family.

About a year after I tried to get pregnant, a miracle happened. About five days after my fifth attempt to get pregnant, I noticed changes in my body. A week later, I took a pregnancy test. When I saw that the pregnancy test was positive, I danced around my house, celebrating the miracle that had just occurred.

Pregnancy is supposed to be a joyful time full of sentiment and warm emotions. However, that is not always the case for abuse survivors. Once I started my fifth week of pregnancy, triggers emerged. I began feeling out of control in my body. I noticed that the depression was creeping back in, and I started feeling undeserving of being pregnant. I had only shared the news with Dorothy and some very close friends. I was terrified of having a miscarriage, due to my history of pregnancy losses during my abuse.

I was diagnosed with a genetic clotting disorder early in the fertility process. I revealed my medical history to the fertility doctor, and she evaluated me for a clotting disorder that is genetic. She told me that if I had not spoken up about my abuse history, I may have never been able to carry a pregnancy to term. The treatment for this disorder required me to inject blood thinners twice a day for the entire pregnancy.

At first, I was elated that I had gotten pregnant, and I had no issue giving myself injections. I noticed a shift around the sixth week of my pregnancy. I had flashbacks when I looked at the bruises on my legs and belly from the needles. I had flashbacks of being injected with drugs during my abuse. As I injected myself with heparin, I remembered what I felt in my body when drugs were put into my body as a child.

As I moved further into my first trimester, I had more flashbacks of when I was pregnant as a teenager. I sobbed in Dorothy's office as I told her I could no longer deny that I was pregnant as a teen. I had proof now. The symptoms of my pregnancy as a thirty-nine-year-old were no different from when I was fifteen, sixteen, or eighteen. My belly felt the same. My breasts were tender. I had headaches every day. I was gaining weight.

Like many survivors of childhood abuse, pregnancy triggered fear and shame. We need to do a lot of work to manage these feelings and deal with triggers that we had not confronted before a pregnancy.

Triggers during a Pregnancy

1. You may not be excited about the pregnancy. Feelings of detachment and numbness are common.

2. If the pregnancy was unplanned, that can result in feelings about prior assaults as a child.

3. Even though society says pregnancy is a time of joy and excitement, it can also be complicated. At times it can be

scary and shame inducing. All your feelings about pregnancy are valid, and there is no right or wrong way to react.

4. You may feel like you are losing control over your body. A growing belly or other bodily functions or the baby's movement in your belly can induce fear and shame.

5. You may worry excessively about losing the baby, especially if you feel undeserving of being pregnant by choice.

6. Dissociation is common during pregnancy. This might be your brain's way of defending against memories associated with your abuse in childhood.

7. You may experience flashbacks when you are meeting with your OB/GYN. You may feel distrusting and resistant to having vaginal examinations.

8. Giving birth can be retraumatizing. Having conversations with your partner or doctor weeks before giving birth will help manage these triggers.

9. Many of us may find pregnancy to be healing and empowering.

Routine prenatal care and exams with doctors and medical personnel can trigger memories of abuse, cause flashbacks, and trigger the fight, flight, or freeze response. Research indicates that women with a history of abuse experience higher levels of fear and anxiety. Body therapies, including massage or body work, help women feel more control over their bodies. Survivors also report that doing yoga helps them to ward off dissociation.

It is important to note that survivor dads can experience PTSD symptoms as they watch their partners go through pregnancy. There may be times when survivor dads feel helpless and out of control as the pregnancy progresses. It can be especially difficult during childbirth because that can remind survivor dads of feeling powerless and out of control during their abuse experience.

Pregnancy can also trigger feelings of abandonment. Many of us have had to go on with our lives, without the support of our parents, siblings, or adults who hurt us growing up. We need to think about how to develop a tribe of supporters and accept that many of these people may not be biologically related to us.

During my pregnancy, I started forming a network of support because I knew that as a single parent, I was going to need to ask for help at times. I talked at length with Dorothy about my feelings about not having my parents in my life once my baby boy was born. I cried about it. I journaled about it. I talked to close friends and colleagues a lot! All of them reassured me that it is okay to bring a child into this world, who may not have grandparents or biological family members as an integral part of their lives. They reminded me that it is not the biological connection that matters. Dorothy told me often that I was going to have many more feelings about not being able to give my baby boy grandparents. She reiterated that he would not know any different because he never met my parents. I needed to take this time to grieve another loss as a result of my abuse history.

Parenting infants and small children makes the strongest people lose it at times. Babies and toddlers have no concept of boundaries or need for down time. How many times have you sat down to dinner and seconds later your infant started crying? How many times have you been in public, and your toddler started screaming bloody murder as if you were torturing them? Taking care of infants and toddlers is an adjustment for any new mother.

Navigating the needs of your precious baby or toddler can be especially difficult for childhood abuse survivors. Things like diaper changing, bath times, and breast feeding can trigger feelings of invasion, intrusion, and fear. Managing the needs of your child, while containing memories and feelings from childhood, requires a lot of patience, building coping strategies and space to process what is emerging in your mind and body.

If you can recognize and place the feelings as one of the effects of the abuse itself, you can separate the memories. Instead of focusing on what you are most afraid of, you can focus on what is different. For example, when I was parenting my little guy as an infant, I observed how I acted toward him. When I changed his diaper, I felt sad and scared for my younger self, and I affirmed my ability to parent after what happened to me. When my little guy had meltdowns, usually in front of others, I watched myself react to him. I told myself hundreds of times that setting boundaries and being firm was not abusive. I thought about all the conversations I had with Dorothy about becoming a parent. I promised myself that if I felt triggered or out of control in my emotions with my little guy that I would ask for help. There were dozens of times when I felt overwhelmed as a single parent or out of control with the changes as my little guy developed. Just hearing from others that these feelings were normal and that the changes I experienced were appropriate helped me keep my feet on the ground.

As our children grow up, we are confronted with a number of challenges that no therapy session or book can prepare us for. That old saying that as children get bigger, they have bigger issues has a lot of merit! One of the most difficult challenges as parents is when our children reach the age when our abuse began. These are experiences we cannot avoid. The best thing we can do to take care of ourselves is talk about it! Cry about it! And remind ourselves hundreds of times that we broke the cycle of abuse. We did not let what happened to us stop us from doing the hardest job in the world—parenting.

Actionable Steps to Manage Triggers as Parents

- When kids are hitting or screaming, step away and ask your partner for help. Talk with your partner about what you are feeling. Do not beat yourselves up for needing space when your children are yelling or hitting to try and get your attention. If you cannot step away from the situation because you are worried about your children's safety, grab a pillow or something for your child to yell at.

- Use communication to create safety and connection. Rather than yelling back you can say things like "Words are not meant to hurt people" or "I feel angry when you yell at me."

- When little ones go from being super happy to distressed over the course of seconds, that can trigger unpredictability with their parents' anger. Remind yourselves that adults have choices about how they react, but children look to us to teach them how to express any uncomfortable feelings, including anger.

- Pay attention to your child's triggers, so you can be better prepared when they may start to act out or be aggressive. It is okay to redirect your children or take a time out if the emotions of that moment feel too big to confront.

- You may notice that you feel angry when your children's needs get in the way of things you have planned for yourselves. This can be especially difficult for people who felt emotionally neglected or abandoned. There may be a part of you that feels angry when you need to tend to your children. That does not make you selfish. It is normal to feel angry when you recall times in your childhood when your parents or other trusted adults did not give you the attention you needed. Instead of shaming yourself for feeling angry, plan a time later that day or week when you can do self-care or get together with grown-ups.

- One of the most painful triggers for many of us is not having dependable grandparents when we become parents. There may be times when you need to grieve for this loss. It is also important to think about what you will say to your children if they start asking who their grandma or grandpa is. Children are curious and they ask questions all the time. It is best to tell the truth in a way that makes sense to them developmentally. One day out of the blue, when my little guy was around eight years old, he asked me, "Are your parents dead?" He was aware that his friends had grandparents, and he noticed he did not have that. There is no right or wrong way to answer this question. I decided to answer his question over time. When he first asked me, I told him that my dad passed away years ago and that my mother was not in my life because she was not a nice person. He was satisfied with that answer. As he gets older and understands more about trauma and abuse, we will have conversations about my biological family.

DISCOVERING INTIMACY AFTER ABUSE

A history of complicated childhood abuse can predict many challenges with romantic relationships. Our emotions from the abuse are unpredictable and at times out of proportion to what is happening in the moment. At any moment reminders of our abuse can be triggered, especially when we are trying to form intimate relationships in adulthood. We must work extremely hard not to externalize or internalize or dissociate from our reactions. Internalizing happens when we try to control our emotions in silence. Externalizing behaviors are when we direct our feelings onto the other person. Disassociation is our way of trying to leave our body when experiencing feelings associated with our past. These learned behaviors are ineffective in adult relationships because they are defense mechanisms and the feelings in that moment do not match the present. That can leave the adults with whom we are trying to connect confused and pushed away.

Most of us have spent years trying to protect ourselves from others. We want to have healthy relationships and partners, but our distrust in human connection has affected those bonds. That does not mean we cannot have intimacy. It means that we need to work ridiculously hard in therapy or with our support system to face our fears and break down our defenses, so we can be vulnerable and form a deep connection.

The first step to forming an intimate relationship is to tell our partner that we have a history of trauma from childhood. We can share as little or as much as we want with our partner. Many of my clients have shared their histories with their partners over the course of time. Some talk about it in bits and pieces. Other clients have come into session with their partners and disclosed in the session more specific things about their past.

I was working in therapy with one client in her early thirties—let's call her Cassie. She started therapy with me when she was eighteen years old. Prior to starting therapy with me, Cassie went to an inpatient facility that treated eating disorders. While she was there, she opened up a bit about her abusive childhood. At that time, she still lived with her parents.

Cassie described her mother as a narcissist, and she told me her dad had "anger management issues." She reported incidents when her father became physically abusive when she was in elementary school. Cassie talked at length about her mother's pathology and the harm it caused to her sense of self. From an early age Cassie reported that her mother was hyper critical of her weight. On numerous occasions, Cassie said that her mother ridiculed her for eating and often told her to lose weight, even though she did not have a weight problem. Cassie was a competitive athlete up until her eating disorder became so severe, she could no longer play sports.

When I met Cassie, she was quiet, sad, and extremely anxious. She was insecure about everything from what she looked like, to how she sounded, to worrying excessively about disappointing others. When Cassie started therapy with me, she had a boyfriend. They started dating when she was sixteen years old. I thought it was odd that Cassie did not talk a lot about him in our sessions. At times I probed, asking questions like "How has it been going with Chad?" She would answer generically, saying things are good.

I noticed that when I did ask about her and Chad, she would lose eye contact with me, and her voice became very shaky. I sensed she was holding some type of secret. At that time, I assumed her timidness was more about her relationships with her parents.

About two years after we started therapy, Cassie opened up about her relationship with Chad. I will never forget this one time when we had a session and Cassie started hysterically crying, telling me things with Chad were really bad. She told me about incidents when he verbally, physically, and sexually abused her. Cassie kept saying, "I want to break up with him, but I am so afraid of what he will do."

It took Cassie three times to break up with Chad and stay broken up. For about six months she would end things with Chad and then go back to him a couple of weeks later. Part of Cassie's healing required her to look at the abuse being done to her and link those experiences to patterns with her parents.

Once Cassie said goodbye to Chad, her healing from childhood took off. She was able to talk more openly about her parents' treatment of her. She reported multiple times when her dad hit her and her mother verbally berated her, usually in public. Over the course of four years, Cassie moved out of her house, and she received her graduate degree in nursing. She was financially and emotionally independent of her parents. The wounds caused by the abuse done to her by Chad and her parents was the focus of her treatment.

When Cassie turned twenty-five years old, she decided she wanted to start dating. She was set up with a couple of different men through friends. Cassie was terrified of making a connection with a male. Very reluctantly, she went on some dates, but she was unable to be present and let her guard down. Instead of giving up, Cassie continued to work through feelings of shame and fear.

One day Cassie came into my office and before she even sat on the sofa, she announced, "I met someone." I had never seen Cassie look so happy. Her eyes were glowing as she described Jonathan's personality. Cassie dated Jonathan for about three months before mentioning him in our sessions. At first Cassie was ambivalent about forming another intimate connection, fearing she would attract another person who was emotionally or physically abusive.

As the months went by, and Cassie continued to explore her feelings with Jonathan, she built more trust in herself and in Jonathan. Cassie opened up more about her history of abuse growing up. She had several conversations with Jonathan about specific incidents of abuse and the impact that it had on her life into adulthood. When Cassie talked to me about these discussions with Jonathan, she reflected on his reaction and responses.

During one session, Cassie shared that Jonathan was so different from her former boyfriend and interactions she had with her parents growing up. She said Jonathan was caring, compassionate, and patient. She told me that when she felt uncomfortable during intimacy, Jonathan was able to tolerate her boundaries and show genuine concern.

It was incredibly moving to witness the transformation in Cassie as she became closer to Jonathan. She became more confident, more trusting, and much more open to the idea that intimacy was possible after surviving childhood abuse. Two years after they began dating, they got engaged. When Cassie came back to therapy after her wedding and honeymoon she told me, "My relationship with Jonathan has proved to me I can be vulnerable, and I now believe there are safe people in this world." Cassie continued to come to therapy during their first year of marriage. We talked at length about the steps she could take to create safety when she was triggered. She gave herself space with Jonathan and for herself in therapy to work through challenges that arose because of being married.

Actionable Steps to Healing in an Intimate Relationship

- Identify and understand how to regulate your emotions when you are triggered.

- Track your feelings and write them down in a journal. Ask yourself what happened before, during, and after the event that ignited a negative reaction.
- Pay attention to patterns of feelings.
- What is the narrative you tell yourself that leads you to feel a certain way?
- Write down how you handled these emotions. Think about the first time you felt this way and try to identify what is it about now versus the past.
- Think about where you stored these emotions in your body.

Creating Safety with Your Partner

- Talk to your partner about what you are working on in your healing.
- Consider sharing your emotions and what triggers came up that day.
- Be open to letting your partner help you identify different ways of responding to these emotions.
- Let your partner provide you with different ways to react when you are triggered.
- Work with your partner on creating safety. Give examples of what safety would include. Ask for validation, or an acknowledgment, of what happened in the past and how that affects you in the present.
- Work with your partner on using physical touch or eye contact to connect.
- If certain types of touch are triggering, share that with your partner. Offer different ways your partner can show affection through physical touch or sexual contact.

Different Modalities You Can Use to Heal in an Intimate Connection

- Go to therapy and do some body work or EMDR for repetitive triggers.
- Meditate and work on breathing strategies to calm your nervous system.
- Spend time in nature and focus on keeping your body present and connected to the earth.
- Consider using holistic medicine tools, such as acupuncture, reiki, or naturopathic supplements.
- Think about doing yoga or some type of exercise alone and with your partner.
- Communicate with your partner during sex, and after sex tell them what did or did not work.
- Take your time and give your body a chance to feel aroused. If feelings of shame, guilt, or fear come up during that part of intimacy, talk with your partner or your therapist.
- Set boundaries and be clear that they may change from moment to moment, depending on what feelings get activated.

Dear Reader,

It takes courage and strength to sit down and read a book about childhood abuse. For years, I would tell people, "I cannot imagine being a childhood abuse survivor." I did whatever I could to stay in denial and separate myself from the truth. When I saw books about related topics, I would brush right past them and think awful thoughts.

Now that you have completed this book, I would like to offer words of support and encouragement to you, whether you are a survivor, a loved one of a survivor, a therapist, or advocate for adults who have been abused as children. While I know there are parts of this book that are hard to sit with, I am hoping that you walk away with messages of healing, hope, and determination. For years, I believed that people "like me" could never live a full life. I believed that I was damaged goods and that my dad "ruined me." I assumed that I would never make it into my adulthood because the pain of my past would be impossible to face and work through.

I waited to write this book until I was ready to speak the full truth about my past. I waited to write this book until I had proof that it is possible to be a parent and have intimacy and safety in relationships with others. If you are struggling with the idea that you can thrive after abuse, you have taken an enormous step by reading about others who are on a similar path to you.

Reading a book does not cure C-PTSD. Reading a book about surviving childhood abuse does not lessen the pain or impact of what you have been through. But taking steps to own your experience and allow yourselves to know the full impact will help you live a safer, fuller, and happier adulthood. When I served as an expert witness on behalf of plaintiffs who have been abused as children, I told the judge that C-PTSD is a life-long condition that cannot be cured. Speaking the truth and finding ways to love and comfort ourselves when we are triggered or grieving allows us to make choices that are about love and safety. Instead of shaming ourselves or thinking our lives can never be "normal," because of what happened to us, we can choose to make choices that do not replicate our past. We can choose to set boundaries, take time to grieve, and implement self-care and self-love. We can choose to talk in therapy or reach out to close loved ones when our triggers are getting in the way of being present. We can choose to accept who we are and know that we are much more than a survivor of childhood abuse. We are also other people's friends, loved ones, coworkers, advocates, and parents.

These are statements I tell myself everyday:

1. I am worthy.
2. I am lovable.
3. I am caring.
4. I am strong.
5. I am determined.
6. I am a fighter.
7. I am grateful.
8. I am free.
9. I am safe.
10. I am healing.

Acknowledgments

This book would not have been possible without the courage and determination of the hundreds of clients I have met throughout the last twenty-seven years. Their stories, the pain, the fight, the heartache, the triumph, and the healing I have witnessed in therapy with clients inspire me every single hour I sit down for another session. It was not until I became a therapist that I realized there are many other people out there who understand the shame, isolation, and fear that comes with facing our history of childhood abuse. On countless occasions, I have driven home from my office wanting to write this book in the hopes that survivors could have a resource that instills hope and guidance in this crazy-making recovery process. It takes tremendous courage to step foot into a therapist's office, and every time clients break their silence in therapy, I am humbled by their trust and courage. My work as a therapist is much more than a job. It is an opportunity to take years of my own pain and horror and find ways to help others flip the horror into hope, meaning, and full living.

Throughout the last few decades, I have met some incredible colleagues and trauma specialists that have played a key role in my work as a therapist and my own journey of facing my history of childhood abuse. I am blessed to have met Dr. Jane Shure and Dr. Beth Weinstock, after I started my first job as a counselor immediately after I received my master of social work. I met them at a conference where they presented a life-changing workshop on shame. At that time, I was repressing my abuse; I was barely hanging on to the idea of living, as I was battling with severe PTSD. I reached out to both of them after I attended their workshop. I believe that meeting them was the first step, in my late twenties, to breaking my silence in therapy about being sexually abused by my father.

Two years before I broke my silence about being an abuse survivor, I started seeing my therapist, Dorothy Saynisch. I met her months after I attended Jane and Beth's workshop. I spent over ten years in intensive therapy with Dorothy, trying to make sense of years of buried shame and pain associated with my abuse. Dorothy was the rock I never had growing up. She was the first adult I allowed myself to trust and be vulnerable with. She taught me the meaning of boundaries, and she helped me understand what I needed to feel safe in connections with other people. I thought of Dorothy every time I sat down at this computer to write another page of *Stolen Childhoods*. When the words I put down on paper felt triggering or too painful to sit with, I thought of things Dorothy told me. I imagined her sitting down next to me as I wrote this book. I believe that Dorothy helped me save my own life. I have internalized my connection to Dorothy, and I know I could not have written this book without her.

Early in my healing process, I met an incredible woman, Sandy Joy Weston. She came into my life around the same time I started working through years of incest, betrayal, and abandonment by my parents. When I met Sandy, I had no idea that she too had experienced a multitude of traumas early in her life. For years, Sandy owned a gym, and I was a devoted fitness class member. Sandy was much more than a fitness instructor. She was a beam of light that helped me stay sane and keep fighting, no matter how much I wanted to give up during my recovery. Sandy has become the big sister I always wanted. She was in the room when I gave birth to my buddy boy, Andrew. Sandy inspired me to pursue my dream of publishing a book. She helped me believe that anything is possible and that dreams can come true.

A few years after I opened my private practice for psychotherapy, I met another incredible colleague, Dr. Heidi Cooperstein. We have been working together on behalf of clients for over twenty years. Heidi is so much more than a colleague I share clients with. She is one of the kindest, most caring women I have ever met. I will never forget when she reached out to me days after I had surgery for thyroid cancer. She reassured me that all would be okay, and she helped me feel less alone and less ashamed about having cancer. She helped me understand that my cancer was not related to me breaking my silence about my abuse. Throughout the past twenty years, I have texted and called her hundreds of times when I am having flashbacks or when I feel overwhelmed, personally or professionally. It was not until I met Heidi that I believed that there are therapists and psychiatrists out here that really do care. She is also like the big sister I never had. She has stood by me throughout the writing process, and she reminds me that the pain will pass. This book would not be possible without her love and support.

Throughout the last twenty-seven years, I have met and joined forces with so many inspiring and caring colleagues, journalists, and advocates who have helped me grow personally and professionally. They have supported me in using my voice and given me opportunities to share messages of hope and healing on a variety of platforms. I am so grateful for my connection with Dr. Liz Kuh, Harin Feibish, Karen Eselson Belding, Judy Rabinor, Rennik Soholt, Reena Friedman, Chelsea Damberg, Kate Snow, Ali Gorman, Denise Nakano, Janice Baker-Kinney, Dyer Pace, Bill Hinkle, and so many more!

I would also like to acknowledge members of my tribe who have encouraged me and supported me in my career as a therapist and an author. During the last twelve years, after giving birth to my buddy boy, I have met some incredible families. These friends have been a source of light and fun! They have stood by me, even at some of my darkest moments. I love you Shkedy family, Bell family, Silverman family, Seltzer family, Horton family, and Angstadt family. You have made life so much more valuable and each of you has played an integral role in my healing. Everyone needs a tribe of supporters and people to turn to when life becomes overwhelming.

Lastly, I would like to thank my book agent, Linda Konner, without whom this book would not be possible. She believed in me and helped me find an amazing publishing house, Rowman & Littlefield. I am so grateful to you for giving me this opportunity to share years of growth, meaning, understanding, and healing, and the means to share that with survivors all throughout the world.

Resources

Online Resources for Adult Survivors of Childhood Abuse

Adult Survivors of Child Abuse (ASCA): An international self-help support-group designed for adult survivors of physical, sexual, and/or emotional abuse or neglect.

https://www.ascasupport.org

Help for Adult Victims of Child Abuse (HAVOCA): HAVOCA was established in 2001 to provide support and direction to any adult who has experienced child abuse. This experience may be firsthand, as a loved one of a survivor, or as a support worker for the victims of child abuse. The HAVOCA resource provides a wealth of information online and at the same time allows people to connect through the HAVOCA Survivor Forums. In doing so, HAVOCA provides direction and friendship to survivors worldwide.

https://www.havoca.org

Rape, Abuse, and Incest National Network (RAINN): About the National Sexual Assault Telephone Hotline | RAINN. The largest anti–sexual violence organization.

https://www.rainn.org

National Association of Adult Survivors of Child Abuse (NAASCA): NAASCA addresses issues related to childhood abuse and trauma. They educate the public to help society get over its taboo of discussing childhood abuse. NAASCA also offers hope and healing by providing many services to adult survivors of child abuse and information for anyone interested in prevention, intervention, and recovery.

https://www.naasca.org

Childhelp National Child Abuse Hotline: The Childhelp National Child Abuse Hotline is funded by individuals and companies and serves the United States and Canada. The hotline is staffed twenty-four hours a day and offers crisis intervention, referrals, social services, and support resources.

https://childhelphotline.org

Psychology Today: Find a therapist in your state that specializes in treating PTSD, depression, anxiety, and issues related to childhood abuse.

https://www.psychologytoday.com

Survivorship: For survivors of ritual abuse, extreme mind control, and torture.

https://www.survivorship.org

Stop the Silence: Stop Child Sexual Abuse Inc.: Comprehensive programming with awareness, education, outreach, training, and policy reform.

https://www.ivatcenters.org

TREATMENT PROGRAMS

Mclean Hospital: Mclean is the largest neuroscience and psychiatry program of any private psychiatric hospital in the United States.

https://www.mcleanhospital.org

The Princeton House: A women's trauma program designed to help women understand the impact of trauma in their lives. In this program, women are encouraged to understand the relationship

between their symptoms, their coping strategies, and their trauma history.
https://www.princetonhcs.org

Sheppard Pratt: One of the nation's leading mental health facilities providing help through every step of the recovery process.
https://www.sheppardpratt.org

The Refuge: The Refuge is a trauma and PTSD treatment center focused on holistic rehab and co-occurring addictions, depression, anxiety, and eating disorders. It offers all levels of care, including inpatient. Premier Trauma Treatment Center for Adult Survivors of Childhood Sexual Abuse | The Refuge
https://therefuge-ahealingplace.com

Silvermist Recovery: Our trauma-focused residential treatment program, located on a serene, private campus in southwestern Pennsylvania, focuses on the whole person rather than addressing one specific issue or behavior. By focusing on increasing psychological flexibility, reflection and resilience, clients can achieve symptom reduction, behavior modification, improved functioning, and increased overall well-being.
https://www.silvermistrecovery.com

Timberline Knolls: "Our mission is to offer innovative care solutions for the development of emotionally strong, personally responsible, and socially resilient girls and women. We are committed to maintaining a safe, nurturing environment where each girl or woman can benefit from superior individualized treatment provided by experienced professionals with relentless compassion and an unconditional joyful spirit."
https://www.timberlineknolls.com

The Sanctuary at Sedona: A thirty-day minimum, residential, alternative, holistic childhood sexual abuse inpatient treatment center. At the Sanctuary, we offer a complete healing journey that takes place in a safe environment. We understand trauma and the needs you have as someone who's been traumatized. As such, we make sure to actively involve you and empower you to make decisions about your treatment process.

https://www.sanctuary.net/trauma/childhood-sexual-abuse

NOTES

INTRODUCTION

1. Mahita Gajanan, "'It's Your Turn to Listen to Me.' Read Aly Raisman's testimony at Larry Nassar's Sentencing," *Time Magazine,* January 19, 2019, https://time.com/5110455/aly-raisman-larry-nassar-testimony-trial, accessed January 31, 2023.

CHAPTER 1

1. "Preventing Child Abuse and Neglect," Center for Disease Control, Preventing Child Abuse and Neglect, 2022, https://www.cdc.gov/violenceprevention/pdf/can/CAN-factsheet_2022.pdf.

2. Casey L. Brown, Musa Yilanli, and Angela L. Rabbitt, "Child Physical Abuse and Neglect," StatPearls, NCBI Bookshelf, *National Library of Medicine,* June 14, 2022, https://www.ncbi.nlm.nih.gov/books/NBK470337.

3. A Courageous Voice, "Risk Factors and Child Sexual Abuse," LibGuides at West Sound Academy, https://irp.cdn-website.com/19994dec/files/uploaded/CSA%20Risk%20Factors%20Statistic%20PDF.pdf, accessed March 9, 2023.

4. Iml Lo, "3 Ways Narcissistic Parents Can Abuse Children," *Psychology Today,* May 4, 2022, https://www.psychologytoday.com/us/blog/living-emotional-intensity/202205/3-ways-narcissistic-parents-can-abuse-children.

5. Better Help Editorial Team, "12 Long Term and Short Term Effects of Child Abuse and Neglect to Watch For," Betterhelp, December 22, 2022, https://www.betterhelp.com/advice/abuse/12-long-and-short-term-effects-of-child-abuse.

6. "Is it ADHD or Child Traumatic Stress," The National Child Traumatic Stress Network, August, 2016, https://www.nctsn.org/sites/default/files/resources/is_it_adhd_or_child_traumatic_stress.pdf, accessedMarch 9, 2023.

7. "Is it ADHD or Child Traumatic Stress."

8. Marylène Cloitre, Chris R. Brewin, Jonathan I. Bisson, Philip Hyland, Thanos Karatzias, Brigitte Lueger-Schuster, Andreas Maercker, Neil P. Roberts,

and Mark Shevlin, "Evidence for the Coherence and Integrity of the Complex PTSD (CPTSD) Diagnosis: Response to Achterhof et al. (2019) and Ford (2020)," National Library of Medicine, April 3, 2020, pp. 1 and 11, https://www.ncbi.nlm.nih.gov/pmc/articles/PMC7170304.

CHAPTER 2

1. "Child Abuse Protection Laws." Darkness to Light: End Child Sexual Abuse, https://www.d21.org/get-help/reporting/protection-laws, accessed February 1, 2023.

2. Scott Cacciola and Victor Mather, "Larry Nassar Sentencing: 'I Just Signed Your Death Warrant,'" *New York Times*, January 24, 2018, https://www.nytimes.com/2018/01/24/sports/larry-nassar-sentencing.html, accessed February 5, 2023.

3. Bessel A. van der Kolk, J. Christopher Perry, and Judith Lewis Herman, "Childhood Origins of Self-Destructive Behavior," *American Journal of Psychiatry* 148, no. 12 (December 1991): 1665, https://eqi.org/p1/abuse/vanderkolk_childhood_origins_of_self_destructive_behavior_1991.pdf; and Lauren A. M. Lebois, Meiling Li, Justin T. Baker, et al., "Large-Scale Functional Brain Network Architecture Changes Associated with Traum-Related Dissociation," https://ajp.psychiatryonline.org/doi/full/10.1176/appi.ajp.2020.19060647.

4. Van der Kolk et al., "Childhood Origins of Self-Destructive Behavior."

CHAPTER 3

1. Francine Shapiro, *Eye Movement Desensitization and Reprocessing (EMDR) Therapy: Basic Principles, Protocols, and Procedures*, 3rd edition (New York and London: Guilford Press, 2017).

2. Shapiro, *Eye Movement*.

3. Alexander L. Chapman, "Dialectical Behavior Therapy: Current Indications and Unique Elements," *Psychiatry (Edgmont)* 3, no. 9 (September 2006): 62–68, National Library of Medicine, https://www.ncbi.nlm.nih.gov/pmc/articles/PMC2963469, accessed June 16, 2023.

4. "Internal Family Systems Therapy," *Psychology Today*, May 2, 2022, https://www.psychologytoday.com/us/therapy-types/internal-family-systems-therapy.

5. Peter A. Levine, *Trauma and Memory: Brain and Body in a Search for the Living Past: A Practical Guide for Understanding and Working with Traumatic Memory* [Kindle edition] (Berkeley, CA: North Atlantic Books, 2015).

CHAPTER 4

1. Alessio Maria Monteleone, Orna Tzischinsky, Giammarco Cascino, Sigal Alon, Francesca Pellegrino, Valeria Ruzzi, and Yael Latzer, "The Connection between Childhood Maltreatment and Eating Disorder Psychopathology: A Network Analysis Study in People with Bulimia Nervosa and with Binge Eating

Disorder," *Eating and Weight Disorders* 27, no. 1 (March 28, 2021): 253–61, National Library of Medicine, https://www.ncbi.nlm.nih.gov/pmc/articles/PMC8860810, accessed August 25, 2023.

2. Bessel A. van der Kolk, J. Christopher Perry, and J. L. Herman, "Childhood Origins of Self-Destructive Behavior," *The American Journal of Psychiatry* 148, no. 12 (December 1991): 1665, https://pubmed.ncbi.nlm.nih.gov/1957928/.

3. Van der Kolk et al., "Childhood Origins of Self-Destructive Behavior."

4. Bessel van der Kolk, *The Body Keeps the Score: Brain, Mind, and Body in the Healing of Trauma* (New York: Viking, 2014).

5. "Sexual Abuse and Addiction: Unraveling a Complex Relationship," Edwards Henderson Lehrman [blog], August 19, 2022, https://www.epllc.com/sexual-abuse-addiction-unraveling-complex-relationship, accessed August 25, 2023.

6. "Linking Childhood Trauma and Addiction in Adulthood," Silvermist Recovery, September 11, 2018, https://www.silvermistrecovery.com/2018/09/2019-guide-the-link-between-childhood-trauma-and, accessed August 25, 2023

7. "Understanding Childhood Trauma," Safe and Sound Treatment, Childhood Trauma and Addiction: The Connection Explained, https://safesoundtreatment.com/childhood-trauma-and-addiction, accessed August 25, 2023.

Chapter 5

1. Jeremy Sutton, "Shame Resiliency Theory: Advice from Brené Brown," Positive Psychology, April 26, 2023. https://positivepsychology.com/shame-resilience-theory.

2. Brené Brown, *Atlas of the Heart: Meaningful Connection and the Language of Human Experience* (New York: Random House, 2021), https://www.amazon.com/Atlas-Heart-Meaningful-Connection-Experience/dp/0593207246.

3. Jeremy Sutton, "Empathy in Counseling: How to Show Empathetic Understanding," Positive Psychology, August 8, 2017, https://positivepsychology.com/empathy.

4. Brené Brown, "3 Things You Can Do to Stop a Shame Spiral," YouTube, https://www.youtube.com/watch?v=TdtabNt4S7E, accessed April 26, 2023.

5. Beverly Engel, "Healing the Shame of Childhood Abuse through Self-Compassion," *Psychology Today*, January 15, 2015, https://www.psychologytoday.com/us/blog/the-compassion-chronicles/201501/healing-the-shame-of-childhood-abuse-through-self-compassion.

6. Kristen Neff, quotes from the author of *Self-Compassion: The Proven Power of Being Kind to Yourself* (New York: HarperCollins [S.I.], 2011), https://www.goodreads.com/author/quotes/4559299.kristen_neff, accessed April 26, 2023.

7. Neff, quotes from *Self-Compassion*.

CHAPTER 6

1. Becky Upham, "Childhood Trauma May Lead to Anger in Adulthood," Everyday Health, March 31, 2023, https://www.everydayhealth.com/emotional-health/childhood-trauma-may-lead-to-anger-in-adulthood.

2. Jennifer J. Freyd, "Definition of Betrayal Trauma Theory," University of Oregon, September 16, 2022, https://scholarsbank.uoregon.edu/xmlui/bitstream/handle/1794/65/defineBT.html;sequence=1.

3. Sandra P. Thomas, Sarah C. Bannister, and Joanne M. Hall, "Anger in the Trajectory of Healing from Childhood Maltreatment," National Library of Medicine, December 14, 2011, 169–80, https://www.ncbi.nlm.nih.gov/pmc/articles/pmc3361676.

4. Catherine Riessman, *Narrative Methods for the Human Sciences* (Thousand Oaks, CA: Sage Publications, 2007).

5. Peter Walker, *The Tao of Fully Feeling: Harvesting Forgiveness Out of Blame* (Scotts Valley, CA: CreateSpace Independent Publishing, 2015).

6. Walker, *The Tao of Fully Feeling.*

7. Walker, *The Tao of Fully Feeling.*

CHAPTER 7

1. Janina Fisher, *Healing the Fragmented Selves of Trauma Survivors: Overcoming Internal Self-Alienation* (New York: Routledge, 2017), 217, https//www.amazon.com/Healing-Fragmented-Selves-Trauma-Survivors/dp/0415708230. For a definition of "attachment," see *Psychology Today*, https://www.psychologytoday.com/us/basics/attachment.

CHAPTER 8

1. Jorunn E. Halvorsen, Ellen Tvedt Solberg, and Signe Hielen Stige, "To Say It Out Loud Is to Kill Your Own Childhood: An Exploration of the First Person Perspective of Barriers to Disclosing Child Sexual Abuse," Science Direct 113 (June 2020), https://www.sciencedirect.com/science/article/pii/S0190740919312745.

2. RAINN, May 2023, https://www.rainn.org, accessed May 11, 2023.

CHAPTER 9

1. Christine Courtois, *Complex Trauma*, Psych Alive, https://www.psychalive.org/wp-content/uploads/2012/08/FINAL-Glendon.ComplexTrauma.Overview-and-Update.-06-12.pdf, accessed June 21, 2023.

2. Courtois, *Complex Trauma.*

3. Angela Haupt, "Why Is Everyone Working on Their Inner Child?" *Time* magazine, April 6, 2023, https://time.com/6268636/inner-child-work-healing/.

BIBLIOGRAPHY

A Courageous Voice. "Risk Factors and Child Sexual Abuse." Accessed March 9, 2023. https://irp.cdn-website.com/19994dec/files/uploaded/ CSA%20Risk%20Factors%20Statistic%20PDF.pdf.

Better Help Editorial Team. "12 Long- Term and Short-Term Effects of Child Abuse." Betterhelp, December 22, 2022 (updated August 11, 2023). https://www.betterhelp.com/advice/abuse/12-long-and-short-term-effects-of -child-abuse/.

Botwin, Shari, quoted in Angela Haupt. "Why Is Everyone Working on Their Inner Child?" *Time magazine*, April 6, 2023. https://time.com/6268636 /inner-child-work-healing/#:~:text=Inner%20child%20work%20can %20also,both%20positive%20and%20negative%20emotions.

Brown, Brené. *Atlas of the Heart: Meaningful Connection and the Language of Human Experience.* New York: Random House, 2021. https://www.amazon .com/Atlas-Heart-Meaningful-Connection-Experience/dp/0593207246.

Brown, Brené. "3 Things You Can Do to Stop a Shame Spiral." YouTube (2 min., 15 sec.). Accessed April 26, 2023. https://www.youtube.com/watch?v =TdtabNt4S7E.

Brown, Casey L., Musa Yilanli, and Angela L. Rabbitt. "Child Physical Abuse and Neglect." National Library of Medicine, June 14, 2022 (updated May 29, 2023). https://www.ncbi.nlm.nih.gov/books/NBK470337/.

Cacciola, Scott, and Victor Mather. "Larry Nassar Sentencing, I Just Signed Your Death Warrant," *New York Times*, January 24, 2018. Accessed February 5, 2023. https://www.nytimes.com/2018/01/24/sports/larry-nassar -sentencing.html.

Chapman, Alexander. "Dialectical Behavioral Therapy: Current Indications and Unique Elements." National Library of Medicine. Volume 3 (2006): 62– 68. Accessed June 16, 2023. https://pubmed.ncbi.nlm.nih.gov/20975829/.

"Child Abuse Protection Laws." Accessed February 1, 2023. https://d2l.org/get -help/reporting/protection-laws/.

Cloitre, Marylène, Chris R. Brewin, Jonathan I. Bisson, Philip Hyland, Thanos Karatzias, Brigitte Lueger-Schuster, Andreas Maercker, Neil P. Roberts, and Mark Shevlin. "Evidence for the Coherence and Integrity of the

Complex PTSD (CPTSD) Diagnosis: Response to Achterhof et al. (2019) and Ford (2020)." National Library of Medicine. *European Journal of Psychotraumatology* 11, no. 1 (April 3, 2020). https://www.ncbi.nlm.nih .gov/pmc/articles/PMC7170304/.

Courtois, Christine. "Complex Trauma." Training. PsychAlive. Accessed June 21, 2023. https://www.psychalive.org/wp-content/uploads/2012/08/FINAL -Glendon.ComplexTrauma.Overview-and-Update.-06-12.pdf.

Engel, Beverly. "Healing the Shame of Childhood Abuse through Self-Compassion." *Psychology Today*, January 15, 2015. https://www .psychologytoday.com/us/blog/the-compassion-chronicles/201501/ healing-the-shame-of-childhood-abuse-through-self-compassion.

Fisher, Janina. *Healing the Fragmented Selves of Trauma Survivors: Overcoming Internal Self-Alienation*. New York: Routledge, 2017. Page 217.

Freyd, Jennifer J. "What Is a Betrayal Trauma? What Is Betrayal Trauma Theory?" University of Oregon, September 16, 2022. https://dynamic.uoregon .edu/jif/definebtl.html.

Halvorsen, Jorunn E., Ellen Tvedt Solberg, and Signe Hjelen Stige. "To Say It Out Loud Is to Kill Your Own Childhood: An Exploration of the First Person Perspective of Barriers to Disclosing Child Sexual Abuse." Science Direct. *Children and Youth Services Review* 113 (June 2020).

Iml, Lo. "3 Ways Narcissistic Parents Can Abuse Children." *Psychology Today*, May 4, 2022. https://www.psychologytoday.com/us/blog/living-emotional -intensity/202205/3-ways-narcissistic-parents-can-abuse-children.

"Internal Family Systems." *Psychology Today*, May 2, 2022. https://www .psychologytoday.com/us/therapy-types/internal-family-systems-therapy.

"Is It ADHD or Child Traumatic Stress." The National Child Traumatic Stress Network, August, 2016. Accessed March 9, 2023. https://www.nctsn.org/ sites/default/files/resources/is_it_adhd_or_child_traumatic_stress.pdf.

Lebois, Lauren A. M., Meiling Li, Justin T. Baker, et al. "Large-Scale Functional Brain Network Architecture Changes Associated with Traum-Related Dissociation." Pyschiatry Online. *The American Journal of Psychiatry*, September 25, 2020. https://ajp.psychiatryonline.org/doi/full/10.1176/appi .ajp.2020.19060647.

Levine, Peter, and Bessel A. van der Kolk. *Trauma and Memory: Brain and Body in a Search for a Living Past*. Berkeley, CA: North Atlantic Books, 2017.

"National Institute of Justice." Home | National Institute of Justice. Accessed March 9, 2023. https://nij.ojp.gov/.

Neff, Kristen. Quotes from the author of *Self-Compassion: The Proven Power of Being Kind to Yourself*. New York: HarperCollins [S.I.], 2011. Accessed April 26, 2023. https://www.goodreads.com/author/quotes/4559299 .kristen_neff.

"Preventing Child Abuse and Neglect." Center for Disease Control, 2022. https: //www.cdc.gov/violenceprevention/pdf/can/CAN-factsheet_2022.pdf.

RAINN. May 2023. Accessed May 11, 2023. https://www.rainn.org.

Riessman, Catherine. *Narrative Methods for the Human Sciences*. Thousand Oaks, CA: Sage Publications, 2007.

Shapiro, Francine. *Eye Movement Desensitization and Reprocessing (EMDR) Therapy: Basic Principles, Protocols, and Procedures*. New York: Guilford Publications, 2018.

Sutton, Jeremy. "Shame Resiliency Theory: Advice from Brene Brown." Positive Psychology, April 26, 2023. Published June 14, 2017, by Jeremy Sutton. https://positivepsychology.com/shame-resilience-theory.

Thomas, Sandra P., Sarah C. Bannister, and Joanne M. Hall. "Anger in the Trajectory of Healing from Childhood Maltreatment." National Library of Medicine. *Archives of Psychiatric Nursing* 26, no. 3 (December 14, 2011). Pages 169–80. https://www.ncbi.nlm.nih.gov/pmc/articles/pmc3361676/.

Upham, Becky. "Childhood Trauma May Lead to Anger in Adulthood." Everyday Health, March 31, 2023. https://www.everydayhealth.com/emotional-health/childhood-trauma-may-lead-to-anger-in-adulthood.

Van der Kolk, Bessel A., J. Christopher Perry, and Judith Lewis Herman. "Childhood Origins of Self-Destructive Behavior." *The American Journal of Psychiatry* 148, no. 12 (December 1991). https://eqi.org/p1/abuse/vanderkolk_childhood_origins_of_self_destructive_behavior_1991.pdf.

Walker, Peter. *The Tao of Fully Feeling: Harvesting Forgiveness Out of Blame*. Scotts Valley, CA: CreateSpace Independent Publishing, 2015.

INDEX

abandonment, 35–37, 66, 84, 90, 151; fear of, 85
Abducted in Plain Sight, 17
abuse: actionable steps after, 23–24; breaking the silence, 15–22; disclosure of, 118; dissociation management, 28–29; flashback management, 24–28; ownership of, 106; in parents, 48, 94; reenactments of, 132; remembrance of, 15–32; reporting of, 113; safety of recovery, 29–32; verbal, 41. *See also* child abuse; childhood abuse
abuser, survival bond with, 99
acceptance, of grief, 65, 93, 129
acknowledgment, 117, 134
acupuncture, 159
addiction: alcohol, 51, 61–62; behaviors, 60; drugs, 51; eating disorder and, 52–62; gambling, 57; sex, 57; steps to heal from, 61–62

ADHD. *See* attention deficit hyperactivity disorder
adoption, 148
adult, trusted, 97–98
adverse childhood experiences, 21
advocate, 84; self, 109
affirmations, positive, 161
alcohol, 65, 87, 122; addiction, 51; dependency, 4, 49
alcoholism, 61–62
American Journal of Psychiatry, 20
American Psychiatric Association, 36
amygdala, 6
Angelou, Maya, 15
anger, 5, 19, 57, 113, 133; accessing of, 81–95; actionable steps for, 87–88; alternative outlets for, 114; displaced, 82–83; emotions connected to, 85–88; expressing of, 91; of indignation, 83; journaling and, 87; management,

104; drawing of, 97–109; emotional, 98; establishment of, 101–2; formed in childhood, 97; guilt and, 104–9; healthy, 97, 101, 105, 109; holding the line, 97–104; identification of, 104; ignoring, 4; importance of, 98; infractions with, 97; judgment of, 108; lack of, 100; with parents, 102–3; physical, 97; pre-determined, 104; reasons for, 109; reframing thoughts of, 108; relationship, 100; respect for, 4, 112; self-care and, 105; setting of, 12, 103, 159; shift in, 106; types of, 97; using your voice for, 105–9; violation of, 97–99
breast feeding, 151
breathing strategies, 27, 91, 159
Brown, Brené, 69, 173n2, 173n4
bruises, 2
bulimia, 52, 55, 67, 93. *See also* eating disorder
bullying, 7, 74, 116
burns, 2
butterfly hug, 142

cancer, 6, 65, 115, 147–48

CAPTA. *See* Child Abuse Prevention and Treatment Act
caregivers, 47
caretaker, 33
CBT. *See* Cognitive Behavioral Therapy
chemotherapy, 65, 106, 115
child abuse: cause of, 16; cycle of, 145, 152; death from, 1; effects of, xiv; emotional, 4–5, 19; generational, 93, 145; gifts, 17; history of, ix; impact of, xii, xiv; memories of, ix, xiii; neglect, 6; physical, 1–2; from positions in authority, xiii; recognition of, 20, 22; secret, 16; sexual, 2–4; statistics, 1; threats, 17; unimaginable, 112
Child Abuse Prevention and Treatment Act (CAPTA), 15
childhood, lost: actionable steps after, 69; grieving of, 63–79; self-compassion and, 72–79; shame and, 69–72
childhood abuse, ix; accounts of, 112; adult survivors of, 117; CPTSD, 8–14; effects of, 81; emotional, 4–5; forms of, 1–14; history of, 111; impact of, 111; intimacy after, 154–57;

114–15, 124, 159; guilt and, 65; management of, 12; pain and, 164; pillars of, 69–70; self-compassion and, 75–76; spiral, 70; toxic, 90; unresolved, 148

Shapiro, Francine, 36, 172n1, 172n2

silence: actionable steps after, 23–24; barrier to, 111; breaking of, 15–22, 127; suffering in, xiii

skepticism, 112

sleep, 91; disruption, 2

smoking, 87

social isolation, 4

social media, 17–18; limiting time on, 31

socioeconomic status, 1

somatic experiencing (SE), 43

somatic flashbacks, 10

startle response, 118

stigma, 114

subpersonalities, 41

substance abuse, 4, 29, 49, 65; disorders, 40, 47, 57, 60; National Institute on Drug Abuse, 51; in parents, 51

suicidal ideation, 12, 41, 118–20

suicide, 38; attempts, 2, 8, 12, 48; tendencies, 26, 65

support: group, 56, 113; network, 117, 135, 151; for partners and friends, 117–25; for survivors, 125; system, xiii, xvi, 14, 23, 56, 154

survival bond, 99

survival mode, 52

Surviving R. Kelly, 17

survivors, xvi, 35; adult, 117; disbelieved, xiii; doubt in, 111; resources for, 112; secondary, 113; speaking out, 111

talk therapy, 42

tapping technique, 28

temper, 82–83

therapeutic modalities: DBT, 33–35; EMDR, 33–35; IFS, 33–35; in recovery, 36–42, 44–46

therapeutic strategies, xiii

therapist, trauma-informed, 45–46

therapy, x; BetterHelp, 6, 171n5; CBT, 38; DBT, 38–41; equine-assisted, 62; group, 39, 62; outpatient, intensive, xii; pet, 31, 86, 91, 93, 146; talk, 42; trauma, 13, 89; years in, xiv

toilet-training accidents, 2

trauma: childhood, xiv–xv; history of, x, 113, 155; processing of, 127;

About the Author

Shari Botwin, LCSW, has been counseling survivors in recovery from all types of traumas in her Cherry Hill, New Jersey, private practice for over twenty-eight years. Her second book, *Thriving after Trauma: Stories of Living and Healing*, was published in 2019. Botwin has served as an expert witness in high-profile cases related to abuse and sexual assault. In July 2022, Botwin presented a webinar for the Trauma and Recovery Institute in China on the role of eating disorders in staying stuck in childhood abuse. Botwin has conducted keynote presentations for continuing education credits for Advanced Recovery Systems, Stockton Institute, and Rutgers University. Botwin has given expert commentary on breaking stories related to trauma on a variety of international outlets, including *NBC Nightly News with Lester Holt*, *Good Morning America*, *NBC News Now*, *CBS This Morning*, the *New York Times*, *Rolling Stone*, *Parents*, *Sports Illustrated*, and others. Botwin lives outside of Philadelphia with her twelve-year-old son and two cats.